L'Auberge espagnole

Part romantic comedy, part sitcom, part social drama, *L'Auberge espagnole* (*The Spanish Apartment*) recounts a familiar 'youth' ritual – the move from university to 'the real world', the often complicated personal, romantic and cultural encounters that ensue, and the moral uncertainties that characterize that key biological and physiological developmental stage between adolescence and adulthood. French director Cédric Klapisch showcases the extraordinary color and beauty of Barcelona's architecture, and places his hero Xavier at the heart of this smartly written film, which makes a series of wry observations on educational exchange programmes, multi-culturalism, and the direction European youth might take in the twenty-first century.

This book addresses the topic of Europe's youth generation, paying particular attention to the ways in which the film depicts the transition from adolescence to adulthood as allegory for the experiences of European society as it moves through periods of readjustment towards uncertain futures. It also looks into the ecosystem of contemporary French cinema, the Erasmus programme and its influence on youth experience, and identity politics in relation to 'nationhood' and 'European-ness'. The book also examines the two sequels to the film – *Russian Dolls* (2005) and *Chinese Puzzle* (2013) – to reveal how the complications faced by the main characters across the trilogy suggest that the move to adulthood is a never-ending process of growing up and reaching a level of self-actualization.

Ben McCann is Associate Professor of French Studies at the University of Adelaide. He is the co-editor of *Michael Haneke: Europe Utopia* (Columbia UP, 2011) and *Framing French Culture* (Adelaide UP, 2015) and the author of *Ripping Open the Set: French Film Design, 1930–1939* (Peter Lang, 2013), *Le Jour se lève* (I.B. Tauris, 2013), and *Julien Duvivier* (Manchester UP, 2017).

Cinema and Youth Cultures
Series Editors: Siân Lincoln & Yannis Tzioumakis

Cinema and Youth Cultures engages with well-known youth films from American cinema as well the cinemas of other countries. Using a variety of methodological and critical approaches the series volumes provide informed accounts of how young people have been represented in film, while also exploring the ways in which young people engage with films made for and about them. In doing this, the Cinema and Youth Cultures series contributes to important and long standing debates about youth cultures, how these are mobilized and articulated in influential film texts and the impact that these texts have had on popular culture at large.

Clueless
Lesley K. Speed

Grease
Barbara Jane Brickman

Boyhood
Timothy Shary ˙

Easy A
Betty Kaklamanidou

The Hunger Games
Catherine Driscoll and Alexandra Heatwole

L'Auberge Espagnole
European Youth on Film
Ben McCann

For more information about this series, please visit: www.routledge.com/Cinema-and-Youth-Cultures/book-series/CYC

L'Auberge espagnole
European Youth on Film

Ben McCann

Figure FM.1 Official poster for *L'Auberge espagnole*

Image courtesy of Alamy

LONDON AND NEW YORK

First published 2018 by Routledge

2 Park Square, Milton Park, Abingdon, Oxon, OX14 4RN
605 Third Avenue, New York, NY 10017

Routledge is an imprint of the Taylor & Francis Group, an informa business

First issued in paperback 2020

British Library Cataloguing-in-Publication Data
A catalogue record for this book is available from the British Library

Library of Congress Cataloging-in-Publication Data
A catalog record for this book has been requested

ISBN: 978-1-138-68122-4 (hbk)
ISBN: 978-0-367-73453-4 (pbk)

Typeset in Times New Roman
by Apex CoVantage, LLC

For Jen

Contents

Figures and table

Figures

Table

Series editors' introduction

Despite the high visibility of youth films in the global media marketplace, especially since the 1980s when Conglomerate Hollywood realized that such films were not only strong box office performers but also the starting point for ancillary sales in other media markets as well as for franchise building, academic studies that focused specifically on such films were slow to materialize. Arguably the most important factor behind academia's reluctance to engage with youth films was a (then) widespread perception within the Film and Media Studies communities that such films held little cultural value and significance, and therefore were not worthy of serious scholarly research and examination. Just like the young subjects they represented, whose interests and cultural practices have been routinely deemed transitional and transitory, so were the films that represented them perceived as fleeting and easily digestible, destined to be forgotten quickly, as soon as the next youth film arrived in cinema screens a week later.

Under these circumstances, and despite a small number of pioneering studies in the 1980s and early 1990s, the field of 'youth film studies' did not really start blossoming and attracting significant scholarly attention until the 2000s and in combination with similar developments in cognate areas such as 'girl studies'. However, because of the paucity of material in the previous decades, the majority of these new studies in the 2000s focused primarily on charting the field and therefore steered clear of long, in-depth examinations of youth films or was exemplified by edited collections that chose particular films to highlight certain issues to the detriment of others. In other words, despite providing often wonderfully rich accounts of youth cultures as these have been captured by key films, these studies could not have possibly dedicate sufficient space to engage with more than just a few key aspects of youth films.

In more recent (post-2010) years a number of academic studies started delimiting their focus and therefore providing more space for in-depth examinations of key types of youth films, such as slasher films and biker films or examining youth films in particular historical periods. From that point on, it was a matter of time for the first publications that focused exclusively on key youth films from a number of perspectives to appear (*Mamma Mia! The Movie*, *Twilight* and *Dirty Dancing* are among the first films to receive this treatment). Conceived primarily as edited collections, these studies provided a multifaceted analysis of these films, focusing on such issues as the politics of representing youth, the stylistic and narrative choices that characterize these films and the extent to which they are representative of a youth cinema, the ways these films address their audiences, the ways youth audiences engage with these films, the films' industrial location and other relevant issues.

It is within this increasingly maturing and expanding academic environment that the **Cinema and Youth Cultures** volumes arrive, aiming to consolidate existing knowledge, provide new perspectives, apply innovative methodological approaches, offer sustained and in-depth analyses of key films and therefore become the 'go to' resource for students and scholars interested in theoretically informed, authoritative accounts of youth cultures in film. As editors, we have tried to be as inclusive as possible in our selection of key examples of youth films by commissioning volumes on films that span the history of cinema, including the silent film era; that portray contemporary youth cultures as well as ones associated with particular historical periods; that represent examples of mainstream and independent cinema; that originate in American cinema and the cinemas of other nations; that attracted significant critical attention and commercial success during their initial release and that were 'rediscovered' after an unpromising initial critical reception. Together these volumes are going to advance youth film studies while also being able to offer extremely detailed examinations of films that are now considered significant contributions to cinema and our cultural life more broadly.

We hope readers will enjoy the series.

Siân Lincoln & Yannis Tzioumakis
Cinema & Youth Cultures Series Editors

Acknowledgments

I would of course like to thank Yannis Tzioumakis and Siân Lincoln for initially commissioning this book and for their immense patience, guidance, and advice as it was being written. I have known Yannis for a number of years, and he has always been a valuable mentor and firm friend.

My thanks too to Lisa Campbell, who conducted useful research work on the film for me during her time in Paris.

The Faculty of Arts at the University of Adelaide has been very supportive of this project and granted me a period of study leave in the second half of 2017 in order to complete the book.

As always, my very special gratitude goes to Jacqueline, and to Monty, Cleo, and Marlowe. They know this film now.

Author's note: all translations from French into English are my own, unless stated otherwise.

Introduction

It's always sunny in Barcelona

I'm French, Spanish, English, Danish. I'm not one, but many. I'm like Europe,
I'm all that. I'm a real mess.

(Xavier, *The Spanish Apartment*)

It's a sentimental education by way of MTV's 'The Real World' by way of
Benetton.

(Hornaday 2003)

Released in the summer of 2002, *L'Auberge espagnole/The Spanish Apartment*[1] is a French-Spanish coproduction written and directed by the French
director Cédric Klapisch.[2] It tells the lighthearted story of Xavier (Romain
Duris), a rather straitlaced, callow French student who spends a year in
Barcelona as part of the Erasmus university exchange program and ends up
sharing an apartment with a motley group of fellow Erasmus students drawn
from across Europe. Incorporating dialogue in French, Spanish, English,
Catalan, Danish, German and Italian, *The Spanish Apartment* proposes
a number of manifestations of European identity that gradually emerge
through the comic interplay between cultural comparison, cliché and gentle
stereotype. As Xavier discovers in this 'astonishingly good-natured movie'
(Baker 2003: 935), the similarities that exist among young adults from different European countries far outweigh the differences.

Nominated for six César Awards,[3] including for Best Film and Best Director, and the winner of several 'audience awards' at international film festivals,
The Spanish Apartment remains Klapisch's best-known and admired work. It
sold nearly 3 million tickets in France, and around 5 million across Europe,
and was subsequently distributed widely and enthusiastically embraced by
global audiences. It launched Duris's career, cemented Klapisch's reputa-
tion and was responsible for a 100% increase in Erasmus applications to
Spain the year following its release (Klapisch 2017a). Often sniffy towards

Klapisch, *Cahiers du cinéma* called it 'a blast of fresh air' (Malausa 2002: 86), and *The Washington Post* heralded a film '*about* young people that isn't exclusively *for* young people' (O'Sullivan 2003, original emphasis). Part romantic comedy, part sitcom, part social drama, *The Spanish Apartment* recounts a familiar 'youth' ritual – the move from university to 'the real world', the often complicated personal, romantic and cultural encounters that ensue, and the moral uncertainties that characterize that key biological and physiological developmental stage between adolescence and adulthood. In an apt description of Klapisch's nonchalant style, David Denby described *The Spanish Apartment* as a 'discursive, sketchbook movie' (2003). Indeed, fragmentary both in form and content, the film showcases the extraordinary color and beauty of Barcelona's architecture, and places Xavier at the heart of this humming city hub. But Klapisch also reaches for heftier targets and crafts a smartly written film that makes a series of wry observations on educational exchange programs, multiculturalism, and the direction European youth might take in the twenty-first century.

Though on the surface this sunny, pan-European film might be regarded as a frat-house comedy (as several critics did on first viewing), Klapisch deftly develops other themes as well – alienation, the bitter-sweetness of love, the melancholy of youth, the putting away of childish things – to reinforce his career-long preoccupation with the fraught relationship between

Figure I.1 The magnificent seven: flat-sharing in Spain
Image courtesy of Photofest

individuals and community and the need for universal acceptance and tolerance. Klapisch has been mining this territory since 1992, with his work emphasizing groups of twenty-somethings striving to establish themselves in an increasingly globalized, disconnected world. His earlier films, like *Le Péril jeune/Good Old Daze* (1994) and *Chacun cherche son chat/When the Cat's Away* (1996), also depicted younger characters on the cusp of adulthood, and his later sequels to *The Spanish Apartment – Les Poupées russes/ Russian Dolls* (2005) and *Casse-tête chinois/Chinese Puzzle* (2013) would return a second and third time to the main protagonists to see whether their initial aspirations – both romantic and professional – had been fulfilled. It was no surprise to discover that the Xavier of *Chinese Puzzle*, pushing forty, was no less befuddled and baffled as his younger self a decade and a half earlier. But it is not just Xavier with teething problems. *The Spanish Apartment* is full of sparky, bristling performances from a set of actors many of whom were relatively unknown at the time of shooting, and since 2002, some have gone on to become the most recognizable faces in European art house and commercial cinema. Many of Klapisch's films display the same characteristics, namely, 'sprawling casts, intersecting storylines and a strong sense of place [and] recognizable characters in melodramatic situations that are flecked with drawn-from-life humor as well as a sincere form of light pathos that feels earned' (van Hoeij 2017). As we shall see, *The Spanish Apartment* certainly fits the bill here.

It is worth reminding ourselves of the plot. Xavier is twenty-five, studies economics and lives in Paris with his hippy mother. His father puts Xavier in touch with an old school friend, who tells Xavier that in the expanding Eurozone, fluency in Spanish will guarantee his chances of employment in France's Ministry of Finance. Thus, Xavier spends his final year as a student at the Autonomous University of Barcelona as part of the Erasmus program. After a number of false starts, he ends up sharing an apartment with six other students from six different European countries – Isabelle (Cécile de France, Belgian), Wendy (Kelly Reilly, English), Soledad (Cristina Brondo, Spanish), Lars (Christian Pagh, Danish), Alessandro (Federico d'Anna, Italy) and Tobias (Barnaby Metschurat, German). While in Barcelona, Xavier undergoes a series of personal, emotional and sexual adventures. He meets a French neurologist and has affair with his wife (Judith Godrèche); he splits up from his French girlfriend back in Paris (Audrey Tautou) and begins a tentative relationship with Neus (Irene Montalà), a local. The film ends with Xavier returning to France a changed person – having acquired a much more plural sense of community and self, he sees himself as a foreigner in his own country. Dismayed at the monotony of his new job at the ministry, Xavier quits on day one and decides to become a writer. His first novel is to be called *L'Auberge espagnole* – 'The Spanish Apartment'.

As this synopsis makes clear, the plot corresponds to the familiar rhythms of the 'coming-of-age' genre. Klapisch himself has described the film as the story 'of a Frenchman who becomes a foreigner' (Klapisch 2002c). In other words, *The Spanish Apartment* is a *Bildungsroman* or, rather, a *Bildungsfilm*. It is a 'sentimental education', during which Xavier grows and develops emotionally, learns lessons along the way, leaves adolescence behind and enters a new, adult phase of his life. Xavier's process of formation, his 'becoming European', takes place against the backdrop of one of Europe's most cosmopolitan cities, and Klapisch showcases Barcelona's architecture, easy living and *duende*. Xavier takes part in a range of coming-of-age rituals: studying, making new friends, learning to understand his parents, juggling lovers and learning to talk *puta madre* Spanish from locals in a bar. Though twenty-five, he seems to us still very immature, caught between biological drives and social pressures and, as David Considine (1981) once observed when discussing the central figures in youth films, forever grappling 'with the world of his [sic] present and past in order to formulate the self that will emerge in the future' (136). Xavier is engaged throughout *The Spanish Apartment* in a double narrative of selfhood: one written *for* him by Klapisch and one written *by* him about his time in Barcelona. By the close, as he imagines himself standing on a runway, arms outstretched, Xavier is ready to 'take flight' towards a new, expectant sense of self. What happens to him in the city is therefore crucial in conveying him towards this new stage of maturation.

It is also very funny. Via an approach we can term 'sociological comedy', *The Spanish Apartment* is more than just a PowerPoint presentation of the Erasmus exchange program (even though some of my undergraduate students here in Australia still to this day are disappointed when their own 'year abroad' experiences do not replicate those depicted in the film, and even though the film has been instrumental in enhancing awareness and upping participation in the program across Europe). Klapisch's film is largely about 'cross-cultural communication as a means of seeking wholeness within – and despite – the fissures of contemporary society' (Fallon 2007: 211). Some of these modes of communication are highly comedic and almost slapstick in their nature (the mispronouncing of the word '*fac*', a race-against-time scene, which concludes with two men ending up in the same bed). Brief instances such as these nudge *The Spanish Apartment* towards the coordinated 'setup-and-punchline' structures so ingrained in the American teen movie. Other moments of humor, such as the cultural power of untranslatability, the comic effects of mistranslation, the incongruous representations of reality, and the laugher that emanates from a feeling of superiority, are shrewdly woven into the narrative. But amidst these playful and carefree excesses lie more profound issues at play. *The Spanish Apartment* presents a confused generation seeking to find its place in an increasingly globalized, hyper-connected world, where individual languages, cultures and histories often count for naught. *The Spanish Apartment* advocates the importance 'of erasing boundaries, walls, and stereotypes in order to recognize and embrace the multiplicity of identities' (Blum-Reid 2016: 12). In this sense, the film is profoundly modern in its exploration of the 'New Europe' and the ramifications of global tourism, education, linguistic hybridity and the ebbs and flows of cultural identity. Klapisch asks a potent question: within the supranational apparatus of Europe, which risks de-essentializing identity and individuality, how can we ever 'belong'?

A film of brio and panache, *The Spanish Apartment* is also 'modern' in its structure and form: voiceover, split screen imagery, sped-up footage, overlaid graphics and collage sequences are all deployed to convey a rapid, sophisticated narrative. Cynthia Lucia has described the Klapisch style as a 'vibrancy of pacing, production design, dialogue, and composition that fuses an overarching realist aesthetic with elements of high stylization' (2009). Form and content intersect – the overlapping, multicharacter narratives, the 'world music' soundtrack, the transnational casting and the restless flitting between Barcelona and Paris reflect Klapisch's ongoing engagement with the ramifications of contemporary society. Klapisch and his DP Dominique Colin shot with Sony's new HD24p high-definition digital camera and took advantage of the flexibility that the format allows. The patchwork, pop-art style of *The Spanish Apartment* was absolutely aligned to Klapisch's view of contemporary European youth:

> I think it speaks to the nature of things today. These students are search-
> ing for cohesion amid confusion, both the confusion of the world and
> the confusion of being in your 20s and still trying to figure out what you
> want, what you need, what you care about, and the difference between
> what you thought the world was like and what it's really like.
>
> (Klapisch, quoted in Anon. 2003)

The Spanish Apartment brings to life the formative experiences of young contemporary European citizens in a foreign space and then asks another question: 'What does it mean to be young, and European, at the turn of the new millennium?' As Jacqueline Nacache reminds us, between 1990 and 2000, 'the most remarkable phenomenon that occurred in French cinema was a sudden wave characterized by novelty and youth' (2015: 184). Riding this wave, Klapisch and his avatar Xavier show the trials and tribulations of modern European youth culture against the backdrop of a broader continental project of cohesion and acceptance. On the surface, *The Spanish Apartment* often tacks and jibes towards and away from the screwball comedy,

Figure I.2 Cédric Klapisch on location in Barcelona, summer 2001

Image courtesy of Photofest

replete with fast talk, humorous clichés and exaggerated national personas. But this is no boozy 'Euro-trip' comedy or 'meet cute' rom-com; rather, as one might expect from one of French cinema's most accomplished and literate auteurs, it is an elegant, intelligent, youthfully exuberant rite of passage. In his book *Le Nouvel âge du cinéma d'auteur français* ['The New Era of French Auteur Cinema'] (2008), David Vasse writes that many first-time filmmakers in France have recently chosen 'the young French generation' as the central theme of their films (32). For Vasse, the most interesting of these films 'focus on the plural form [. . .] or the collective story of a community (a group, a band, a tribe, etc.)' and ask the intimate question "Where am I?"' (33). 'To make a film about their generation', concludes Vasse, 'is a clear statement that *this is indeed the moment to do it*, here, now, and in response to an inner necessity' (34, original emphasis). The moment, then, for Klapisch, was at the start of the 2000s. It was time to tell a story about European youth.

Accordingly, the pan-European apartment, with its 'extensive bonding and familial proximity' (McCaffrey and Pratt 2011: 437) and its multiple languages and practices, chaotic and cohesive at the same time, allegorizes the Erasmus program and the ongoing sustainability of a diverse, plurilingual Europe. Just as the inhabitants of the apartment learn to get along, so too, argues Klapisch, must Europe. For at its heart, *The Spanish Apartment* is a nuanced and complex 'youth film' seeded through with anxieties about how a new generation of upwardly mobile, financially comfortable 'emerging adults' (Arnett 2004) will be able to find their place in this new Europe. According to Duris, *The Spanish Apartment* is about 'doing what you want to do and not letting yourself be dictated to by others' (Mereu-Boulch 2002a). The film thus follows a classic teen-movie philosophy: self-determination, stubbornness and anti-establishment posturing. Ever since his first film, *Riens du tout/Little Nothings* (1992), Klapisch has been fascinated by the dynamics and affinities of the group – be it a collection of friends, family, work colleagues or students – and his work explores how those groups interact in times of emotional or economic turmoil. Often, they will fragment or splinter; other times they find unity in diversity. *The Spanish Apartment* falls into the second camp. As one review of the film concluded, Klapisch 'represents a fairly benevolent vision of people of diverse cultural identities and nationalities muddling together and providing one another with mutual support, despite their differences' (Dawson 2003). Its utopian thrust is palpable.

The film's interculturalism is visible at all turns – its co-funding agreement between France and Spain, its shuttling back and forth from Paris to Barcelona, its pan-European cast and its plural languages and musical choices. Thus, in spite of its lighthearted themes, *The Spanish Apartment* in fact engages with fundamental questions about what it means to be Catalan, Spanish, European and/or African, how these various identities are modeled and how they can be synchronized both on an individual and a collective level. For Samuel Amago, Klapisch's central message 'is that Catalonia is not only about Gaudí, the Catalan language and the enjoyment of *pa amb tomàquet* [bread and tomato], it is also a diverse cultural space where Europeans, Africans and multiple other global diaspora mix and intermingle' (2007: 22). That is to say, this is not just a travelogue film; it has something important to say about European youth. With its motto of 'unity in diversity', Europe can overcome its cultural differences and foster a sense of belonging to a European society. With the help of travel-based cross-border programs of the kind shown in *The Spanish Apartment*, interaction among young people – the so-called 'Erasmus generation' – will, in an idealistic sense, serve to strengthen the feeling of European identity.

'Europe is a mess', says Xavier, towards the end of *The Spanish Apartment*. Klapisch's angle on Europe is encapsulated in that one word. Promoting the film in London in 2003, he admitted as much: 'Of course, Europe is a mess. Just as life is a mess. But I try to put a positive spin on the word [. . .] And for me, I like to live in a multicultural, melting pot environment. Because the idea of unifying everything leads to fascism' (Brooks 2003). Thus, the apartment *is* Europe. It is a polyphonic melting pot, an *'auberge espagnole'* that takes pride in its heterogeneity and chaos. It is what Europe – and whether this view is too simplistic or not has been debated ever since the film's release – should be aspiring to. In fact, in a speech to the European Parliament in Brussels in October 2010 about the importance of film

Figure I.3 The Erasmus generation in Barcelona

to European identity, the German director and President of the European Film Academy Wim Wenders ruefully noted that Europe today is largely perceived by its citizens 'as a political-technical-bureaucratic structure, a more or less indistinct economic conglomerate' (2010: 1). Wenders called for European policy makers and politicians to tap into the 'emotional side of Europe' as a way of revitalizing the European project and making it more meaningful and relevant to ordinary people's lives. Cinema, he argued, was the best way to create an emotional bond between Europe and its citizens. European film culture 'tells [. . .] of local and regional stories and conflicts. It is specific, full of local colours and tastes, of accents and languages. It celebrates diversity, even more so: It keeps cultural diversity alive!' (Wenders: 6). Wenders might just as well be describing *The Spanish Apartment* here as a model for the kind of film necessary to enhance to value of the European project and celebrate the range of diversity and multilingualism that Klapisch fixes on. Certainly, the opening and closing moments of the film, set inside the austere Ministry of Finance building in Paris, reflect the oppressive 'political-technical-bureaucratic' mind-set evoked by Wenders. We can only assume that were he not to have gone to Barcelona, Xavier would have easily slipped into the stable, respectable, dreary civil service job offered him by his father's friend. His dreams of being a writer would have quietly ebbed away. Instead, in a sliding-doors moment, Xavier goes to Barcelona, is overwhelmed by Catalonia's 'local colours and tastes [. . .] accents and languages' and returns to Paris a changed man. Not only does the film celebrate cultural diversity in its own right, but it also exemplifies the mobile and multilingual possibilities on offer to Europe's new and emerging youth generation that offer a sunny alternative to the grey, technocratic Europe depicted by Wenders.[4]

Thus in several of the ways mapped out here, *The Spanish Apartment* is a film that reaches powerfully into the twenty-first century. Scholarly and critical interest in Klapisch's film began around 2004–2005, at a time when French cinema was increasingly diversifying and the formerly rather rigid parameters between auteur and popular cinema were beginning to crumble. The ever-changing backdrop of European politics may also have played a part in this newfound engagement with the film's take on alterity, difference and benefits of 'living together'. The film has since been read in a number of different ways: as a critique and a celebration of Erasmus, as an ode to multilingualism and multiculturalism and as a European road movie. For Klapisch, *The Spanish Apartment* is at its heart 'an advertisement for travel [. . .] curiosity and respect' (Brooks 2003). There are other conundrums. Is the film for or against European mobility and youth exchange? Is Klapisch critiquing or celebrating the European project? Are we being asked to sympathize with or show pity to his central protagonist? Why are all the main protagonists white, middle-class and relatively comfortable in their own skin? One of the film's most fascinating aspects is indeed its ever-shifting position on these questions. As we can see, there are multiple, often contradictory forces at play here, and it is the frequent slippage among contrasting readings that typifies the film's complexity and ongoing relevance, not least fifteen years later, when the European project so optimistically proselytized by Klapisch has become increasingly precarious in this post-2008 age of austerity, Brexit, Marine Le Pen and, at the time of writing (December 2017), the ongoing showdown between exiled Catalan president Carles Puigdemont and Spanish leader Mariano Rajoy. By delving once more into *The Spanish Apartment*, our hope is to show how hip European youths, at ease with multiple languages, are Europe's best hope at breaking down barriers of culture, race and stereotype.

Chapter 1 defines the film's relationship to the European youth film and examines the long tradition of films from across the continent that have placed children, adolescents and young adults at the center of their stories. It shows that *The Spanish Apartment* is a *Bildungsfilm* – a coming-of-age film that traces the emotional, moral and sexual development of a young man. It will look more closely at the ecosystem of contemporary French cinema and place *The Spanish Apartment* within a dynamic network of films that privileges youth and youthful behavior and combines the stylistic tenets of auteur cinema and popular cinema. Chapter 2 explores in detail the casting and filming context, production history and reception of *The Spanish Apartment* to better locate it within a broader discourse of ideas around cultural diversity and intercultural relationships. It will also look at the Erasmus scheme and demonstrate how its hyper-modern and pluralized notions, its emphasis on youth and youthfulness and its founding myths of transnational togetherness feed into *The Spanish Apartment* via the mind-sets of the characters. *The Spanish Apartment* also focuses on the negative aspects of Erasmus – linguistic frustration, homesickness, the sense of being lost in a cocoon – while at the same time showing how these perceived downsides are all part of the process of the transition into adulthood undergone by Xavier. Visual style is also important to Klapisch. Just as the film itself keeps stopping and starting in Xavier's head as he (re)composes his opening words to the audience, so too did Klapisch adopt an organic, spontaneous, assemblage-style approach to the project (it was the locations and the cast themselves that informed the direction of the story). It will also look at the various young actors involved in the project: Romain Duris, Cécile de France, Kelly Reilly and Audrey Tautou, all of whom are now established European actors. The chapter will also look more closely at the city of Barcelona itself and examine how it is presented in film as a space of youthfulness, exuberance and fun and is thus perfectly suited as the backdrop for Klapisch's micro-and macro-narratives.

Chapter 3 analyzes *The Spanish Apartment* itself through a series of close sequence analyses (such as the opening scene in Paris and Xavier's arrival in Barcelona) and chart the various ways it incorporates its 'youthful' elements (music, visual style) and presents them to the audience. The chapter will look at the way the film is told – from Xavier's POV, narrated directly to the audience, as if part of a documentary – and the various stylistic strategies (editing tricks, fast cuts, split screens) that reinforce the film's playful and witty approach. Music is also important: the soundtrack ranges from Daft Punk to Radiohead to Chopin to suggest an interplay between tradition and innovation, rhythm and control, classicism and experimentation: all dichotomies that lie at the heart of *The Spanish Apartment* itself and, more obliquely, the European project as evoked by Klapisch. An exploration of the film's inclusive identity politics and stereotypes will highlight the film's positive take on difference, whether in the scene with the Gambian student, who claims that there is no single, valid identity, or in a more broadly humorous way, with the arrival of Wendy's brother William, who spends the rest of *The Spanish Apartment* exaggerating stereotypes and evoking a crass 'little Englander' small-mindedness about the complexities of Europeanness. Finally, the fact that Xavier ends the film by deciding to become a writer rather than an economist suggests that his year in the 'Spanish apartment' was a transformative one, both emotionally and professionally. Chapter 4 briefly examines the two sequels to the film – *Russian Dolls* (2005) and *Chinese Puzzle* (2013) – and proposes that the time-lapse concept and coming-of-age themes in these two films (as characters reminisce about what happened in Barcelona) lead to a greater acceptance of tolerance, diversity and difference. The closing scene of *The Spanish Apartment* sees Xavier recounting for the final time what he went through during his stay in Barcelona – it is done with a sense of longing and introspection, which suggests that the year was one of personal growth and maturation. It is time to turn our gaze to Europe once more.

Notes

1 All references to the film will henceforth be *The Spanish Apartment*. The various nuances of the title will be discussed in Chapter 2.
2 Throughout the 1990s, coproductions among EU member countries became increasingly common, culminating in 2002 with the release of *The Spanish Apartment*.
3 This is the French equivalent of the Academy Awards.
4 Shortly after the release of *The Spanish Apartment*, Klapisch was invited to Brussels by a delegation of European politicians to introduce a screening of the film to the European Parliament.

1   The European youth film

In his still influential *Hollywood Genres: Formulas, Filmmaking, and The Studio System* (1981), Thomas Schatz proposed a set of organizing principles – a 'grammar' – that constitutes a film genre. A system of conventions evolves over time and eventually crystallizes into 'rules' that clearly identify a specific genre. There is a 'network of characters, actions, values, and attitudes' (22) working within either a physical or psychological space. The film genre must simultaneously follow a set, stable formula while allowing external influences – shifting cultural attitudes, economic imperatives, industrial reorganization, new technologies, and so on – to continuously refine and evolve each genre.

In the case of the 'European youth film', what might its 'grammar' be? What are its 'rules'? Can its multiple 'networks' be defined, predicted and replicated? Does it have a 'stable formula'? How has it altered and advanced over time? Given that continental Europe is made up of roughly fifty countries, what does a 'European youth film' look and sound like? Do Albanian or Ukrainian youth films deal with the same types of stories about children, teens and young adults, and if so, what do these similarities tell us about the development of transnational genre in terms of race, ethnicity, sexual difference and history?

The cinematic representation of youth has long been a favored topic for directors. While a great deal has been written about the American teen-oriented film genre, its counter-cultural, rebellious protagonists, its youthful coming-of-age stories, its iconography and characters and its critical place in post-war American film culture (Considine 1985; Doherty 1988; Bernstein 1997; Shary 2005; Driscoll 2011), the analysis of similar genres and stories through the lens of European cinema has only recently begun to be meaningfully conceptualized and theorized. Yet despite its inherent complexity, given the sheer volume of national cinemas involved, and the oft-conflicting aesthetic and formal priorities of individual national cinema styles, the European and the American 'youth film' cohere in several ways. As Catherine Driscoll reminds us, adolescence is an experience that is 'unsettled, uncertain and transitional' (2011: 1). Such moments of hesitancy and 'in between-ness' are not confined to Hollywood protagonists – they appear again and again in contemporary European cinema. As is often the case in American teen cinema, the depiction of young people in European films are generally oversimplified and largely fixed. There are 'safe' characters (innocent, respectful and ideologically neutral), and there is the 'wild child' (anarchistic, disruptive, unruly), and the interplay between these two types may reveal generational and/or institutional divides. As America's cultural landscape evolved, so too did Europe's. The factors behind the rise of the youth film in America were (and still are) mirrored in Europe, such as the emergence of post-World War Two youth culture; the 1960s as a decade of sexual liberation, social disconnect and unease; and cinema's continued targeting of and marketing to new, youthful audiences. Small wonder, then, that the French newspaper *L'Humanité* declared in the opening lines of its review of *The Spanish Apartment* that what was on show was not 'an American Pie' but rather 'a European Paella' (Guilloux 2002). Food analogies notwithstanding, perhaps Klapisch's version of the 'teen film' is actually only a knight's move away from its zeitgeist-defining Hollywood counterpart in terms of target audience and generic pleasures.[1] Sexual frustration and youthful naivety certainly feature in both films.

While scholarly work on the European youth film is a still developing area, three recent studies have mined the genre's ideological complexities and surveyed its stylish formal and visual qualities. Each cuts across national cinemas and offers a fresh pan-European perspective. *Where the Boys Are: Cinemas of Masculinity and Youth* (2005), edited by Murray Pomerance and Frances Gateward, deals with the theme of boyhood and cinematic representations of masculinity. For Pomerance and Gateward, the early part of the twenty-first century is a moment 'when youth dominates all forms of popular culture, and when Western society is structured through an extended adolescence' (2005: 9). Some of the essays focus on teen films from, among others, France and includes a chapter by Patrick E. White on two François Truffaut films – *Les 400 Coups/The 400 Blows* (1959) and *L'Enfant sauvage/The Wild Child* (1970) – both of which feature at their center young males. White notes that at the close of both films, the two boys 'know only that they are stepping into a new world, a world they must make by their rules, that they must invent [which] gives each of them great freedom and joy, but also fear and anxiety' (White 2005: 229). Terms like 'freedom', 'joy', 'fear' and 'anxiety' could be applied to countless coming-of-age stories in European film, and as we shall see in *The Spanish Apartment*, these common themes and emotional responses constantly bubble away under the surface.

Youth Culture in Global Cinema (2007), edited by Timothy Shary and Alexandra Seibel, focuses on several iterations of non-American versions of the teen film in Eastern and Central Europe, Turkey, France, Italy and Spain.[2] Shary and Seibel prefer the term 'youth' rather than 'teen', partly to de-anchor the term from its historicized American context and partly to highlight these films' more sustained engagement with convoluted, thorny issues. As Shary notes in his introductory chapter 'Youth Culture Shock', unlike American teen films, international youth films tend to deal 'with topics of politics and religion [. . .] with tensions around cultural and national identity' (2007: 4). Shary continues in this vein by arguing how European films 'celebrate, and often exploit, the youthful discovery of sex', with central characters 'not only losing their virginity but also questioning their sexual orientation, dealing with pregnancy, and occasionally finding pleasure' (4). He offers a list of characteristic non-American youth films that have received critical attention by virtue of the individual directors' reputations (e.g., *The 400 Blows*, *Ivan's Childhood* [Andrei Tarkovsky, 1962], *Diabolo menthe/Peppermint Soda* [Diane Kurys, 1977], *My Life as a Dog* [Lasse Halleström, 1985] and *Europa Europa* [Agnieszka Holland, 1990]).

In a later chapter, Anikó Imre demonstrates how Hungarian, Slovak and Polish filmmakers have frequently placed children and adolescents at the center of their narratives to stand as representational devices for processing the psychological abuse and social dysfunction to which Soviet control reduced their national citizens during Communist rule. Imre shows how the most common narrative pattern in these post-war youth films was boys' coming-of-age stories (Geza Radvanyi's *Somewhere in Europe* [1947], Miklós Jancsó's *The Bells Have Gone to Rome* [1958] and Jiří Menzel's *Closely Observed Trains* [1966]). For Imre, the actions of the boys in these films universalize a wider theme, namely, the 'ungendered human choices one has to make in situations when youthful idealism pushes against the political constraints of the historical moment' (2007: 72). Youthful idealism is a theme taken up by Daniela Berghahn and Claudia Sternberg in their edited collection *European Cinema in Motion: Migrant and Diasporic Film in Contemporary Europe* (2010). Berghahn and Sternberg focus on feature films dealing with migration and multiculturalism in Europe since the 1980s, and Berghahn's own chapter charts the development since the mid-1980s of a set of European films that deal with the identity struggles of adolescents from ethnic minority backgrounds. She includes British-Asian films (*East Is East* [Damien O'Donnell, 1999], *Bend It Like Beckham* [Gurinder Chadha, 2002]), black British films (*Rage* [Newton Aduaka, 1999], *Bullet Boy* [Saul Dibb, 2004]), plus a long list of Maghrebi-French films like *Le Thé au harem d'Archimède/Tea in the Harem* (Mehdi Charef, 1985), *Le Gone du chaâba/The Kid from the Chaaba* (Christophe Ruggia,

1998) and *L'Esquive/Games of Love and Chance* (Abdellatif Kechiche, 2003). For Berghahn, many of these films conform to the generic patterns of the Hollywood 'teenpic' or 'youth film'.

If, as we shall detail, *The Spanish Apartment* offers a relatively friction-less and fairly settled depiction of youth on film, countless European films have taken different routes. Some explore in far more troubling and vola-tile terms the feelings of awkwardness and dislocated complications that take place during various stages of youth. Ingmar Bergman's *Summer with Monika* (1953) tells the story of nineteen-year-old Harry (Lars Ekborg) and seventeen-year-old Monika (Harriet Andersson), who run away together and spend an idyllic, erotically charged summer on a Stockholm island; *The Spirit of the Beehive* (Victor Erice, 1973) deals with a young Spanish girl's experiences in the early Franco years and her perception of the con-temporary realities of the time through a highly stylized, fantasy lens; *The Edukators* (Hans Weingartner, 2004) looks at youth activism and nonviolent radicalism in Berlin, with its three young protagonists who 'educate' the wealthy elite by breaking into their houses and rearranging their furniture; *LOL (Laughing out Loud)*, a French 2008 film by Lisa Azuelos recounts the trials and tribulations of a teenage girl balancing her life at a prestigious Parisian high school, a burgeoning romance, and a dysfunctional relation-ship with her mother;[3] the main character in Wolfgang Becker's *Goodbye Lenin* (2003) creates a deception (that the Berlin Wall has in fact not fallen, and Communism is alive and well in East Berlin) in order to protect his frail mother, who has recently awoken from a coma; in Sweden, Lukas Moodys-son's diptych *Show Me Love* (1998) and *Lilya 4-ever* (2002) focus on youth-ful figures – in the former, two young girls start a tentative relationship in a dull small town; in the latter, issues of failed parenting, teenage homeless-ness and human trafficking come to the fore as a teenage girl is forced into a prostitution ring in an ex-Soviet republic. Steve Neale notes that the Ameri-can 'teenpic' has always been 'heterogeneous, multi-dimensional and often contradictory in its forms, concerns and modes of address' (2007: 367). As these aforementioned examples make clear, the depiction and representation of youth and adolescence in European cinema are equally compelling in their inventiveness, raw, unadorned honesty, often comic register and above all sensitivity to contemporary social and political realities.

In these films, and many others, the transition from adolescent to adult allegorizes the experiences of society as a whole as it moves through periods of readjustment towards uncertain futures. Many coming-of-age European films deal with the struggle of daily existence against the wider economic and social changes wrought by globalization – themes of poverty, migration, unemployment and the disintegration of the family unit are often recurring background factors here. These points remind us of Jon Lewis's oft-cited argument about the central argument of the teen film in America – that 'despite stylistic, tonal, industrial, and by now even generational differences within the genre, teen films all seem to focus on a single social concern: the breakdown of traditional forms of authority' (1992: 3). The double-edged nature of globalization often comes into play too – on the one hand, Europe's new generation of young people are more mobile, more economically independent and less in thrall to institutional impediments than ever before, but on the other, they make up a new generation of European citizens uncertain about job opportunities, financial comfort and domestic stability as they grapple with the uncertainties of neoliberal economic imperatives and ever-fluid concepts of nationhood, identity and multiculturalism.

Many European directors, especially from France (and we include Klapisch here), have grown up in the aftermath of the 1968 student demonstrations and civil unrest that unfolded across the continent. These new directors exhibit a deep concern for the contemporary social issues mentioned, and European cinema has emerged as an essential space in which the problems of immigration and transnational identity formation have been imagined and contested. Often, the adolescent is cast as a 'hope for the future' to provide an optimistic, utopian safety valve to release the pressure of previous generations and their current social struggles. In *The Spanish Apartment*, Klapisch's youthful protagonists may not be subjected to traumatic life experiences, but the changes that do take place to them are no less momentous. The film's fragmented visual style reflects the increasingly discontinuous essence of modern life, 'punctuated by constant stops and starts, ruptures and breaks, frenzies followed by periods of calm' (Anon. 2003). It is also worth mentioning briefly three other directors at this point: the Mexican trio of Alfonso Cuarón (*Y Tu Mamá También/And Your Mother Too* [2001]), Alejandro González Iñárritu (*Amores perros/Love's a Bitch* [2000]) and Guillermo del Toro (*El espinazo del diablo/The Devil's Backbone* [2001], *El laberinto del fauno/Pan's Labyrinth* [2006]). Though not European, their aforementioned work nonetheless trades in the coming-of-age genre and the tensions brought about by the intensification of globalization. The urgency of their narrative and visual approaches epitomizes how non-American, or perhaps more accurately non-Hollywood, directors continue telling their stories about children and young people in inventive and vital ways, which in turn allegorizes the generational clash between the young and the old (we might productively add to this list Hayao Miyazaki's Studio Ghibli films and Satyajit Ray's *The Apu Trilogy* [1955, 1956, 1959]).

Before turning our attention to France, it is worth concluding these opening remarks by noting the long-standing triangulation between American cinema, the teen movie and Europe as a geographical space. A number of American teen movies and youth films have taken place in Europe, and a recurring aspect of Schatz's 'actions and attitudes' is the figure of the young

American male struggling to adapt to new languages, customs and social rituals in registers that range from the broadly comedic and the 'gross-out' to the horrific and the abject. For Diane Negra, such European misadventure narratives 'highlight the ineptitude and fearfulness of young American males' (2007: 200). Comic road movies like *National Lampoon's European Vacation* (Amy Heckerling, 1985), *EuroTrip* (Jeff Schaffer, 2004) and *Deuce Bigalow: European Gigolo* (Mike Bigelow, 2005) deploy characters who embrace what they regard as the sexual permissiveness and hedonistic licentiousness of European youth culture and are then subsequently cast as strangers in a strange land whose sexual and behavioral mores are at first indulged, then challenged or punished, and then recuperated. In a review for *Russian Dolls*, Stephen Holden noted how Klapisch's young protagonists were 'comfortable in their skins [and] relaxed about sex'. Holden compared his American counterparts less favorably: Xavier, Isabelle, Wendy and the others 'know how to enjoy themselves; their Hollywood peers find it difficult to [. . .] take a deep breath and drink in the moment' (Holden 2006).

Conversely, these narrative trajectories play out to a far more traumatic extent in films like Eli Roth's *Hostel* (2005) and *Hostel: Part 2* (2007). Here, young American backpackers visiting Slovakia are first enticed by a series of beautiful women and then caught up with a shady group of European businessmen who kidnap and torture unsuspecting victims. *Taken* (Pierre Morel, 2008) is not strictly speaking a 'teen movie', although it deploys at its center Kim, the kidnapped daughter of Liam Neeson's ex-CIA operative. He must track her down before she is sold into sexual slavery by Albanian human traffickers. Kim's wholesome 'Americanness' is here brought into direct conflict with a European embodiment of terror and the abject (a dynamic complicated further by the fact that Kim is kidnapped while in Paris, that most quintessential of European cities). Equally compelling in its depiction of an American headlong engagement with European culture is Richard Linklater's 'Before' trilogy (*Sunrise* [1995], *Sunset* [2004], *Midnight* [2013]), featuring a young American (Ethan Hawke) who spends time in Vienna, then Paris, and then the Greek Peloponnese with a French student (Julie Delpy). The film, shot over a period of twenty years, charts the ageing process of the two actors, their shifting perspectives on love (by the third film, they are a couple with children), and themes of self-fulfillment and self-discovery, against the backdrop of European spaces and extended, falling-away tracking shots.

'Adulescents' and 'emerging adults'

Xavier is twenty-five at the start of *The Spanish Apartment*. In France and Spain, where our story takes place, that makes him an adult. But is Xavier *really* an adult? In fact, is *The Spanish Apartment* a 'youth film' at all? It's not a film about children, nor is it a 'teen film'. It does not deploy the typical plots, set pieces or iconography of the teenpic. There are no proms; no one loses his or her virginity; there's minimal drug and alcohol consumption; and familial conflicts take place on the sidelines. It does not take place at school, nor is it about the loss of childhood innocence, juvenile delinquency or teenage rebellion or alienation. The rites of passage here do not involve the humiliating hazing rituals of *Dazed and Confused* (Richard Linklater, 1993). This is not *The Breakfast Club* (John Hughes, 1985) – there are no jocks or nerds, stoners or geeks, princesses or outcasts here, no tear-stained bonding or breaking down of ideological differences and no groups who serve 'as universal representations of youth [. . .] and stand metaphorically against those who resist change' (Charney 1996: 30). They are not adolescents either, at least in the biological sense of the word (the World Health Organization defines this as the period roughly between the ages of 10 and 19). Perhaps they are 'adulescents', a portmanteau term devised by French psychoanalyst Tony Anatrella to designate a portion of young adults who refuse to enter the adult world (1988, 2003). Neither adult nor adolescent, the adulescent is in transition, seeking to establish a new identity. These are young adults who willingly defer the transition to full adulthood, often resort to childlike or regressive behavior and live in and for the present.

For Klapisch, *The Spanish Apartment* and its two sequels chart how Europe's current generation tackles the different stages of the transition from adolescence to adulthood: 'I think people try to be young as long as possible, they try to appear young. Becoming an adult is different today. It's dealing with more responsibility, more a sense of reality' (Hopewell 2014). The main protagonists are university students in their final year of an Erasmus study period, thus putting them roughly in their early twenties. The youngest character in the film is William, Wendy's brother, who shows up midway through the film to spend time in Barcelona with Wendy, and yet the actor Kevin Bishop was twenty-one when filming began. Granted, each of the characters in *The Spanish Apartment* are in the process of self-actualization and are looking towards a future that has not yet been mapped out for them.

In her introduction to *Emerging Adulthood in a European Context*, Rita Žukauskien notes that the transition to adulthood nowadays may include 'finishing formal education, acquiring professional qualifications, getting a permanent job, establishing one's own household, and starting a family' (2016: 4). Such markers, to a greater or lesser extent, apply to Xavier's own development over the course of Klapisch's trilogy, but they are a long time coming. A year in Barcelona is not nearly enough time. As we shall discover, it takes much longer for Xavier to 'become adult'. Though no longer an adolescent at the start of *The Spanish Apartment* (Xavier is not the same as Tomasi, the hedonistic teenager Duris played in an earlier film by Klapisch, *Good Old Daze* [1994]), he seems by choice to be deliberately stuck in between youth and adulthood, immaturity and maturity. This makes his transition from adolescence to adulthood across the trilogy (2002, 2005, 2013) to appear willfully stretched out. He defers the traditional steps towards adulthood while at the same time tries to make sense of his daily experiences within the wider move towards adulthood. The transition is a complex process, often involving multiple steps. In fact, Xavier's prolonged pathway from one status to another is typical of many young people at the start of the twenty-first century.

For Jeffrey Arnett (2004), it is no longer useful to classify people in the 18–29 age bracket as adults because they have often not accepted traditional adult roles (work, marriage, children) by this point. Because young people are deferring such traditional adult markers, they in turn reflect much more on their own lives and achievements up to that point, experiment intensely with their 'in between' status and change their life choices (career, relationships, etc.) rapidly and regularly. This preference instead for a kind of liminal existence that is both distinct and separate from adolescence and adulthood means that young people are no longer compelled to follow the standardized paths of their parents, in part because those traditional life choices can no longer guarantee economic stability or success. Arnett instead proposes the term 'emerging adult', or what he describes as a 'period of development bridging adolescence and young adulthood, during which young people are no longer adolescents but have not yet attained full adult status' (2004: 312).

In *The Spanish Apartment*, these conflicting feelings recur. Xavier undoubtedly feels 'in between'; the black and white photograph of him as a child is often used to trigger a nostalgic glimpse back to Xavier's past, as is the reference to the 'Martine' books that announce a simpler, more clear-cut life. Moreover, Xavier is, at multiple points in the trilogy, free to choose among any number of available life options, whether in Paris, Barcelona, London, St. Petersburg or New York. Already, by the final scene of *The Spanish Apartment*, Xavier's identity has been fragmented and then reassembled into a dynamic new (though still incomplete) version. The star masculinity of Romain Duris here is instrumental in this regard. Tim Palmer includes *The Spanish Apartment* on a list of performances by Duris in the late 1990s and early 2000s that chart his 'growing up on-screen, playing troubled (arrested) adolescents, perennially self-destructive, unable to cope with complex emotions, prone to wild fits of grief-stricken temper' (2015: 423). These simmering modes of masculinity are not as sharply defined or extensive in *The Spanish Apartment* as in other contemporaneous performances by Duris (e.g., *Gadjo dilo/The Crazy Stranger* [Tony Gatlif, 1997] or *Je suis né d'une cigogne/Children of the Stork* [Tony Gatlif, 1999]), and

Figure 1.1   Good Old Daze (1994): Duris, Elbaz and the 'emerging adult' generation
Image courtesy of Photoshot

yet Xavier's young adult torment and his often childlike uncertainty of his place in the world are representative of Arnett's 'emerging adult' figure.

A *Bildungsfilm*

The Spanish Apartment is a coming-of-age film, or a *Bildungsfilm*. The term is borrowed from German literary term *Bildungsroman*, meaning 'novel of formation'. In such novels, made popular during the Victorian era, the subject is 'the development of the protagonist's mind and character, as he passes from childhood through varied experiences – and usually through a spiritual crisis – into maturity and the recognition of his identity and role in the world' (Abrams 1981: 121). The protagonist's passage from childhood to adulthood is often arduous (physically, emotionally, spiritually), and they must often overcome some type of obstacle or navigate some form of moral or ethical crisis in order to develop into adulthood and gain wisdom. The *Bildungsroman* narrates the struggle between the rebellious inclinations of the individual and the conformist demands of society. Examples in the English language include Charles Dickens's *David Copperfield* (1850), D. H. Lawrence's *Sons and Lovers* (1913) and James Joyce's *A Portrait of the Artist as a Young Man* (1916). Finally, the 'getting of maturity' at the close of these novels involves on the protagonist's part some clear recognition of their 'new' identity and their newly acquired self-actualizing role.

Like its literary namesake, the *Bildungsfilm* treats the formative years of its main protagonist(s), their emotional and psychological development, and their learning of a lesson, about life, love and their future. As Lesley Speed defines it, these are films 'set in the past and structured around the protagonist's acquisition of greater maturity [. . .] The acquisition of maturity is equated with greater understanding of past events, and a new capacity to face the future' (1998: 25). Like the novel, the *Bildungsfilm* depicts a series of events, processes and revelations that will have a major bearing on the development of the protagonist. Often clear-eyed and non-sentimental (though not always), this form of coming-of-age story in cinematic terms often falls into the same bracket as the 'teen film' (with its focus on the moral growth from child/teenager/adolescent to adult, often recounted in flashback by an adult narrator) and deals with wider issues of social or political change alongside the moral development of the central character(s). Key Anglo-American *Bildungsfilms* include *American Graffiti* (George Lucas, 1973), *Stand by Me* (Rob Reiner, 1986), *An Education* (Lone Scherfig, 2009), *Boyhood* (Richard Linklater, 2014) and *Moonlight* (Barry Jenkins, 2016); there are also many examples in French cinema, from Truffaut's 'Antoine Doinel' pentalogy (filmed over twenty years with the same lead actor) to Ismaël Ferroukhi's *Le Grand Voyage/The Great Journey* (2004) via Catherine Breillat's harrowing *36 Fillette* (1988) and *A ma sœur!/Fat Girl* (2001), Sébastien Lifshitz (*Presque rien/Almost Nothing* [2000], *Wild Side* [2003], *Plein sud/Going South* [2007]) or Thomas Cailley (*Les Combattants/Love at First Fight* [2014]). Often, these filmmakers do not idealize the transition between youth and adulthood; instead, they focus on the hardships and uncertainties of youth and pose universal questions of identity, self-actualization and subject formation.

Xavier's journey in *The Spanish Apartment* is, to borrow the title of Gustave Flaubert's 1869 *Bildungsroman*, a 'sentimental education', in which an emotional awakening is triggered and the institutional and ideological structures to which he is expected to conform are rejected. On his return to Paris after his year in Barcelona, Xavier soon becomes disillusioned with his new life, quits his job on day one and becomes a writer. His fight to extend the hedonism and freedom he experienced in Barcelona into adulthood forms the backdrop of the next two films of the trilogy. The adventures of his time in the 'Spanish Apartment', enriched by the ease of transnational travel and mobility, can be seen as fitting into what Beck and Beck-Gernsheim call the 'elective', 'reflexive' or 'do-it-yourself biography' (2002: 3), in which 'year abroad' students have the opportunity to explore different ways of being, beyond the more or less fixed patterns of behavior they are required to engage in at home. Across the trilogy, but especially *The Spanish Apartment*, Klapisch depicts youth as a state of being, as a set of psychological processes jammed somewhere between energy and excitement and irresolution and uncertainty. David Stratton, reviewing *The Spanish Apartment* for its Australian free-to-air TV premiere in 2009, wrote pertinently that the film 'very successfully captures the feeling of what it's like to be young, to be sharing accommodation with people your own age – and to be indulging in love affairs, suffering disappointments, discovering soul mates – all the important things of youth' (2009). *The Spanish Apartment* is one of European cinema's great 'what-it's-like-to-be-young' stories because it suggests that – at least for Xavier – coming of age is a constant process, and the act of writing '*The Spanish Apartment*' at the film's end, resulting in Klapisch's repetitive mise-en-scène of books, paper, notes, photographs, keyboards and computer screens, is a means for Xavier to definitively locate a sense of closure. One part of his life ends in Barcelona, and a new beginning is instigated. Ultimately, one of the lasting pleasures of *The Spanish Apartment*, *Russian Dolls* and *Chinese Puzzle* is seeing how Xavier, the youthful friendships he forges over the course of fifteen years, and 'all the important things of youth' evolve hesitantly and haphazardly rather than adhering to a clean, unproblematic transition into adulthood. Like the Erasmus scheme, *Bildungsfilms* are *meant* to be messy.

The Spanish Apartment: interfacing with contemporary French cinema

The Spanish Apartment is a European film in many senses of the word – it's a coproduction between France and Spain that takes place in Barcelona, one of the continent's most cosmopolitan cities. Its myriad of stars is drawn from all quarters of the European Union, and its lingua franca pivots between English, French, Spanish and Catalan. Metaphorically too, it reflects the new terrain of Europe – diverse, mutual, shared, messy and borderless. Yet in its DNA, it is a French film, directed by and starring two of modern French cinema's most inventive, playful practitioners. And so, turning to France, where part of our story takes place, we can anchor *The Spanish Apartment* to a long tradition of films that deal with youthful rebellion, sexual awakening, feelings of hopelessness and displacement, the opacity and ambiguity of the adolescent body and a gnawing sense of disillusionment with the older generation. As we have already hinted at, French cinema has a long tradition of film production that places the impermanence of youth, subject formation and coming-of-age struggles at the center of its stories.

Dominique Thévenin writes in his foreword to Karin M. Egloff's book *Les Adolescents dans le cinéma français: entre deux mondes* (one of the few studies of youthful protagonists in French cinema) that '[t]he adolescent dilemma, its multitude of external determinants and its internal psychological changes have long been a topic of predilection among contemporary French filmmakers'. Ginette Vincendeau lists a number of post-war films that focus on children and adolescents, noting that many of them achieved enormous box office success partly because 'children are innately attractive and they have huge emotional power, able to go from comedy to drama in an instant' (2007: 6).[4] The French New Wave of the late 1950s was celebrated by many not just as the revitalization of old-fashioned and backward-looking filmmaking praxis but also as the harbinger of French modernity and post-war rejuvenation. In *Masculin Féminin/Masculine Feminine* (1966), Jean-Luc Godard used improvised dialogue and an urgent *cinéma vérité* style to capture an intimate, naturalistic overview of French youth on the cusp of the May 1968 protests;[5] Eric Rohmer's urbane comedies of the 1970s and 1980s more often than not dealt with people in their twenties spending time at beaches or seaside resorts (*Pauline à la plage/ Pauline at the Beach* [1983], *Le Rayon vert/The Green Ray* [1986], *Un conte d'été/A Summer's Tale* [1996]).[6] Louis Malle directed a number of films – *Zazie dans le metro/Zazie in the Metro* (1960), *Le souffle au cœur/The Murmur of the Heart* (1971), *Pretty Baby* (1978) and *Au revoir les enfants* (1987) – which concentrated on the children first and their interaction with parents and figures of authority afterwards.

In *Passe ton Bac d'abord/Graduate First* (1978), Maurice Pialat follows a group of post-1968 Lens teenagers in their final year of high school as they prepare to take their *bac*, or *baccalauréat* (final exams), and head out in to the world, uncertain about their future. Young people in Pialat's films were often seen 'as a manipulated, exploited or vulnerable sector of society' (Aitken 2001: 209); here, they engage in casual sex, drift to Paris, seek work and in one key scene, at a wedding, ask an older man, seated next to his wife, about his own marriage. *Were there any others after you got married? – Too many. – Did you love them? – Never. Oh no. No. Never.* The hypocrisy of the parents' generation is held up here for ridicule (as is the teacher who tries to seduce one of his pupils). Back in the early 1980s, Luc Besson, Jean-Jacques Beineix and Leos Carax became the standard-bearers of the *cinéma du look*, a set of films that displayed a spectacular visual style manifested through a highly stylized mise-en-scène (elaborate framing, a preoccupation with decor and color), a cinéphile tendency to reference or recycle from other films and a focus on youthful protagonists who are often marginal or romantic figures (Higbee 2006).

Throughout the 1990s, many French directors turned to youth culture, youth narratives and intimate coming-of-age stories in order to survey the adversities and fears of adolescence in a fast-changing France (see, e.g., Erick Zonca's *La Vie rêvée des anges/The Dreamlife of Angels* [1998], Bruno Dumont's *La Vie de Jésus/The Life of Jesus* [1997] and Noémie Lvovsky's

La Vie ne me fait pas peur/I'm Not Afraid of Life [1999]). More recently, popular comedies like *Neuilly sa mère!/Neuilly Yo Mama!* (Gabriel Julien-Laferrière, 2009), in which a poor teenager from the Paris suburbs spends time in the *haute bourgeoise* world of the capital's richest *arrondissement*, use social inequality as a device to explore sensitive issues of (in)tolerance and multicultural urban harmony, while the *Petit Nicolas* series of films (2009, 2014) adapts a well-loved French story about a young boy and the mischief he gets up to. Christophe Barratier's *Les Choristes/The Chorus* (2004) recounts how an inspirational music teacher transformed the lives of young boys at a boarding school. Both this film, and Barratier's follow-up, *La Nouvelle guerre des boutons/War of the Buttons* (2011), pose numerous questions about what constitutes a good education and a happy childhood and also highlights the ineffectiveness and injustice of discipline, as opposed to compassion and understanding towards the young.

Indeed, French films set in (mainly repressive) schools often pit young against old, chaos against conformity. This tradition dates back at least to Jean Vigo's *Zéro de conduite/Zero for Conduct* (1933), in which a group of rebellious young boys revolt against their teachers and take over the school.[7] While Barratier's films offer conventional depictions of adolescence in their study of rebellion and delinquency, Vigo's far more un-romanticized portrayals of youth have remained an alternative touchstone for contemporary directors. More recently, Bertrand Tavernier's *Ça commence aujourd'hui/It all Starts Today* (1999) and Laurent Cantet's *Entre les murs/The Class* (2008) have used the school setting to shine a light on the dysfunctional state of French society. Finally, *Bande de filles/Girlhood*, Céline Sciamma's 2014 coming-of-age film[8] recounts how sixteen-year-old Marieme (Karidja Touré) must navigate the unsettling transition into adulthood while at the same time struggle against the institutional inequities and disadvantages of being black and living in the underprivileged *banlieues* of outer Paris.[9] The Francophone world has also dwelt on these themes, with the Dardenne brothers and Xavier Dolan placing youth at the heart of their narrative and aesthetic concerns, while North African directors like Moufida Tlatli (*La Saison des hommes/The Season of Men* [2000]), Lyes Salem (*Masquerades* [2008], *L'Oranais/The Man from Oran* [2014] and Merzak Allouache (*Le Repenti/The Repentant* [2012]) evoke child and youth narratives to revisit national and colonial history, interrogate founding myths, and expose current political and religious turmoil.

As we can see, within this flourishing ecosystem of French and Francophone cinema, the *Bildungsfilm* tradition is extensive, often highly political, attracts both popular and auteur filmmakers, and opens up a space for challenging issues and themes to sit alongside comic and nostalgic recreations of adolescence gone by. Adrian Martin notes that 'the teen in a teen movie

[. . .] refers not to biological age, but a type, a mode of behaviour, a way of being' (1994: 66–67). This is certainly true in the case of French 'youth cinema'. Often, the fluctuating transitional state between child and adolescent, or adolescent and adult, allows directors to quarry complex issues such as sexuality, gender roles, family, religion, race and France's *'fracture sociale'* (social divide) and cast those issues into sharp relief against the backdrop of generational struggles between young and old, baby boomer and Generations X and Y (and presumably, sometime soon, Generation Z).

From an industrial perspective too, a number of 'moments' can be pinpointed that signal both the ongoing significance of the French coming-of-age film and anticipate the production contexts and reception of *The Spanish Apartment*. The first is the release of the enormously influential television series *Tous les garçons et les filles de leur âge/All the Boys and Girls of Their Time* in 1994, which sparked a significant contribution to the emergence of a youth-inflected cinema in France. The series, made by the Arte television channel, comprised nine one-hour films by new, emerging and established directors who each took as their starting point a period of the directors' own teenage adolescence and a scene set at a party accompanied by music.[10] This autobiographical series has been regarded by many accounts as a watershed moment in the on-screen depiction of youth culture inside the Hexagon (Austin 2008; Wilson 1999; Mayne 2005). Phil Powrie declared that the series marked the 'attempted return of the auteur' (Powrie 1999: 1),[11] while Judith Mayne noted that because five of the nine directors were women, the series was responsible for kick-starting a new wave of female directors in France (even though Akerman and Denis were already well established by this point). For Mayne, the importance of *Tous les garçons* lies not just in its depiction of female adolescence, but 'female adolescence in relationship to cinematic ways of looking and telling' (Mayne 2005: 210).

Less well-known than *Tous les garçons* but equally as important in showcasing emerging talent in French cinema was another compendium TV series commissioned in 1993 by Arte called *Les Années lycée/High School Years*. This time, four films focused on teenagers about to leave school – *Un air de liberté* (by Eric Barbier), *Attention fragile* (Manuel Poirier), and *Sa vie à elle* (Romain Goupil). The fourth, *Le Péril jeune/Good Old Daze*, was directed by Klapisch and was so well received by television viewers that it subsequently gained a cinematic release a year later. According to Guillaume Soulez, both *Tous les garçons* and *Les Années lycée* offered a moving portrait of mid-1990s French youth, blending 'psychological analysis of the characters and the social and political inscription of the stories with a certain degree of stylistic detachment' (2015: 99). *Good Old Daze* brought Klapisch wider attention, made the careers of 'new' actors like

Romain Duris, Vincent Elbaz, Hélène de Fougerolles and Elodie Bouchez and served as a model for how emerging auteurist filmmakers like Klapisch (he has also written all twelve of the films he has directed) might combine autobiographical memory with stylistic flourish. The influx of new personnel from both projects was a major contribution to the emergence of a new, personal, socially conscious cinema in mid-nineties France.

Second, Judith Franco (2017) has looked at the recent proliferation of young girl/female coming-of-age dramas in European cinema and recognizes the importance of the French format of the genre developed by female directors like Diane Kurys and Catherine Breillat. In the 1970s, both sought to upend traditional representations of young girls to offer more cutting-edge depictions of female subjectivity and to explore the multiple effects that social conventions might have on the formation of female identities. In more recent films, '[a]dolescent girlhood is primarily associated with loss, frustration, and self-estrangement [. . .] that show young women confronted with predatory male sexuality and limited options in their quest to develop a sense of self' (2). Franco's list of French films that are directed by women and offer a child-centered narrative perspective include *Naissance des pieuvres/Water Lilies* (Céline Sciamma, 2007) as well as *Stella* (Sylvie Verheyde, 2008), *No et moi/No and Me* (Zabou Breitman, 2010), *Un poison violent/Love Like Poison* (Katell Quillévéré, 2010), *17 filles/17 Girls* (Muriel and Delphine Coulin, 2011) and *Tomboy* (Céline Sciamma, 2011). These works, and many other European films that deal with a similar subject matter, are frequently 'anchored in self-inscription and marked by a strong focus on the role of lived/embodied experience in girls' identity formation' (2).[12] As we have already suggested, this focus on identity construction and self-actualization is a common motif in European youth film, and in this specific French context, such a focus on the (female) coming-of-age process has thrown up works that are deeply transgressive and thought-provoking.

The ongoing relevance and vitality of these new coming-of-age films outlined by Franco that focused on female subjectivity and were directed by women are part of far broader developments in the (re)presentation of youth and young people in French cinema. The *jeune cinéma francais* ('Young French Cinema') or alternatively the *nouvelle Nouvelle Vague* ('new New Wave') have become a rather ambiguous catch-all 'to designate a new generation of French filmmakers who emerged in the mid-1990s and who concentrated on contemporary issues and often possessed a highly militant streak'. Mayne (2005) describes it an 'elastic term that refers to several generations of post-(and post-post) New Wave film-makers in France of the last decade, whose works are often (but not always) preoccupied with "youth" (another imprecise term)' (207). As already mentioned, many critics saw

Tous les garçons et les filles de leur âge as shepherding a 'new realism' into French cinema and uncovering a group of new auteurs.

Indeed, vast numbers of new filmmakers emerged at this time. Jean-Pierre Jeancolas (2005) has calculated that 470 new filmmakers made their first films between 1993 and 2002. This in turn reinvigorated the domestic industry and allowed new films to focus on hitherto excluded groups and occluded themes. Some read *le jeune cinéma* as a direct response to economic hardship and political upheaval in France (in the mid-1990s, the far-right Front National party made electoral gains – and would again, even more spectacularly in 2002, a few weeks before the release of *The Spanish Apartment*). For Austin (2008), *le jeune cinéma* gives a voice to the excluded and the disenfranchised (i.e., very often French youth) and lends 'a sense of struggle and anger to many of these films' (220). Austin also locates the release of *La Haine/Hate* (1995), Mathieu Kassovitz's pivotal film that traces a day in the life of three marginalized young men from the Parisian *banlieue*, as a key moment in the development and marketability of the genre. Claude-Marie Trémois has listed eight aspects of *le jeune cinema*: urgency, topicality, tight chronology, wandering characters/cameras, improvisation, long sequences, open endings, and a nonjudgmental presentation of the protagonists (Trémois 1997: 47–55). One of the directors included by Trémois in the list of *jeune cinéma* directors was Cédric Klapisch, and several of these characteristics appear in *The Spanish Apartment*.[13]

Third, another catalyst for those French films that placed a greater emphasis on young protagonists (and the young audiences that went to see them) was the emergence of the *comédie d'auteur* (auteur comedy) in the late 1990s. Raphaëlle Moine (2015) characterizes the *comédie d'auteur* as a challenge to the dichotomy that has traditionally existed in France between commercially driven entertainment and high-brow, demanding *auteur* cinema. This genre drives a wedge between the two approaches and styles, opening up an alternative dynamic space where established auteurs might profitably interface with popular genre cinema. Moine includes Klapisch's early comedies (*Little Nothings*, *When the Cat's Away*) as part of this trend and places him alongside such auteurs as François Ozon (*Potiche/Trophy Wife* [2010]) and Alain Resnais (*Pas sur la bouche/Not on the Lips* [2003]). Moine defines this cinematic style as a combination of 'careful, elegant dramatic writing [. . .] a well-constructed plot [. . .] an intimist, autobiographical vein [and] *a polyphonic ensemble form* that interrelates a variety of points of view around a common theme or shared event' (246, my emphasis). Moine might just as well be describing *The Spanish Apartment* here. She concludes by arguing that the register of auteur comedy 'is that of dramatic comedy, which joins the observation of contemporary mores with a 'mixed' form of comedy (in contrast to the laughter and farce of pure comedy)' (247).

Again, in the case of *The Spanish Apartment*, such a coexistence is clearly evident: on the one hand Klapisch deploys wry observations about multi-culturalism and language (the scene in the university lecture theater, the multilingual sign next to the telephone, etc.); on the other, he reverts to the register of a much broader slapstick and the gestures of physical comedy (William-as-a-fly; the race against time as Alistair gets closer and closer to the apartment; William's crass generalisations to the flatmates).

Anticipating some of Moine's later ideas, Tim Palmer had previously suggested that French cinema is increasingly aligning itself to what he terms 'pop art cinema', that is, films that 'flit nimbly [. . .] back and forth between cultural registers high and low. Mainstream pleasures permeate the rarefied materials of the arthouse, as popular and intellectual paradigms intercon-nect, complete osmosis, on-screen' (2011: 97). This model of an overlap between the highbrow and the popular highlights an increasing permeabil-ity in French cinema between auteur-driven films and popular, mainstream genre-driven fare. As the box office figures for *The Spanish Apartment*, *Russian Dolls* and *Chinese Puzzle* indicate, these types of films found increas-ing success in theatres.

Finally, *The Spanish Apartment* forms part of a corpus of French films made in the late 1990s and early 2000s that focus on protagonists leaving their stable homes behind to journey into or across Europe. According to Sylvie Blum-Reid, these extra-hexagonal excursions 'give a vista onto the current landscape of French cinema, and the way it throws bridges to other cultures, countries and cultural practices' (Blum-Reid 2009: 1).[14] Along similar lines, Michael Gott (2015) has written of the growing prominence in contemporary European cinema of 'touring films', which stage encoun-ters and contacts among citizens of different nations. As both filmic process and filmic text, such works engage in and promote – both in narrative and production terms – exchanges among Europeans of different nationalities, cultures and native tongues. In terms of student mobility and Klapisch's enthusiasm for the Erasmus scheme, both Blum-Reid and Gott's formula-tions show how, in the case of *The Spanish Apartment*, encountering other cultures in spaces often far from the protection of the domestic sphere is very much part of the *Bildungsfilm* trajectory. For Klapisch, the border between France and Spain, and by extension, Europe (given France's geographical proximity to several European countries), has become increasingly porous, subject to the ebbs and flows of youthful migration, travel and intercultural journeys of discovery.

As a brief aside, it is worth comparing these immersive and upbeat travel narratives to contemporary French horror films like *Ils/Them* (David Moreau and Xavier Palud, 2006), *A l'intérieur/Inside* (Julien Maury and Alexandre Bustillo, 2007) and *Frontière(s)/Frontier(s)* (Xavier Gens, 2007).

These latter films, all of which feature young or 'emerging adult' protagonists, each share a deep suspicion towards the 'outsider', generally personified by the malicious individual(s) in these films whose motives remain inexplicable, contradictory or pathologically brutal. As such, they serve as a counterbalance to the optimism inherent in films like *The Spanish Apartment*, reflecting as they do a profound skepticism towards the broadening of the European Union and an ingrained fearfulness of the ramifications of flows and movements across and through French borders. Of course, *The Spanish Apartment* does not trade in abject. It regards the 'Other' with curiosity and the amused/bemused eye of the ethnographer. It is not fearful but fascinated. Ultimately, Klapisch's cinema is anthropological insofar as it dissects how communities interact, is drawn to past, present and future cultures and explores how language (both concrete and symbolic) may divide and unite. For his protagonists, travel and border crossings are part of what it means to be a European citizen of the twenty-first century. With that in mind, let us turn to *The Spanish Apartment*.

Notes

1 The original *American Pie* was directed by Paul and Chris Weitz in 1999. To date, there have been seven more sequels and spin-offs.
2 In an appendix titled 'Filmography of Global Youth: Films by Nation', Shary and Seibel list well over 800 'non-U.S. feature films about youth' (2007: 287). The list contains 82 French films.
3 In a neat intertextual twist, the mother in *LOL* is played by Sophie Marceau, who herself played a young teenager struggling to cope with sexuality and peer pressure in Claude Pinoteau's *La Boum/The Party* (1980) and its sequel *La Boum 2/The Party 2* (1982).
4 Vincendeau starts with *Jeux interdits/Forbidden Games* (René Clément, 1952) and ends with *Etre et avoir/To Be and to Have* (Nicolas Philibert, 2002).
5 At the 1966 Berlin Film Festival, the film won the Youth Film Award for 'Best Feature Film Suitable for Young People'.
6 Rohmer once explained that 'people sometimes ask me why most of the main characters in my films are young. I don't feel at ease with older people [. . .] I can't get people older than forty to talk convincingly' (Wakeman 1988: 924).
7 Vigo's film was a direct inspiration for Lindsay Anderson's similarly themed *If . . .* (1968).
8 The title *Girlhood* evokes *Kidulthood* (2006), *Adulthood* (2008) and *Brotherhood* (2016), Noel Clarke's trio of distressing depictions of the young black urban experience in contemporary London.
9 Sciamma was inspired to write the film after she observed groups of young black teenagers on the streets of Paris. She told *Cineuropa*: 'When you meet these girls, they have such energy, such intelligence, such humour, such charisma, even though they don't get to dream a lot and their country does not give them a vision of what they could become or do' (Anon. 2014).

10 The nine directors were: Chantal Akerman, Olivier Assayas, Olivier Dahan, Emilie Deleuze, Claire Denis, Laurence Ferreira Barbosa, Cédric Kahn, Patricia Mazuy and André Téchiné. The time span of *Tous les garçons et les filles de leur âge* ran from the 1960s to the late 1980s, with three films representing each decade.

11 Powrie cites the influence of *Tous les garçons et les filles de leur âge* as one of the three decisive moments in the development of French cinema in the 1990s (the other two are the simultaneous GATT trade negotiations and the emergence of heritage cinema, on the one hand and, on the other, the commitment of French filmmakers to political protest, as indicated by the number of filmmakers (Klapisch included) involved in the protests against xenophobic domestic immigration policies in 1997 (see 1999: 1–21).

12 Other films mentioned by Franco include *Fish Tank* (Andrea Arnold, 2009 [UK]) and *She Monkeys* (Lisa Aschan, 2011 [Sweden]).

13 Other directors mentioned by Trémois included Xavier Beauvois, Arnaud Desplechin, Bruno Dumont and Erick Zonca.

14 *Gadjo Lilo/The Crazy Stranger* and *Exils/Exiles* (2004 – both directed by Tony Gatlif, and both starring Romain Duris) also belong to this trend.

2   *The Spanish Apartment*
Development, production, reception

My job is to observe the people, the settings, and the music of my time. I try
to be a witness to what is taking place around me.

(Klapisch, quoted in Fallon 2007: 202)

To be aged between 20 and 25 years and head off to a foreign country to
study is a life experience that I wish for everyone! You come back completely and utterly changed.

(Klapisch 2002a)

Cédric Klapisch – the 'Europtimist'

As we saw in Chapter 1, Cédric Klapisch, was already, by the time he came to
make *The Spanish Apartment*, a key figure in contemporary French cinema.
Since the film's release in 2002, Klapisch has risen to the apex of the kind
of popular, sophisticated, witty social comedies for which French cinema is
renowned. He has made six films since *The Spanish Apartment* (including
its two sequels); his most recent work – *Ce qui nous lie/Back to Burgundy*
(2017), a mainstream drama about winemaker siblings – has been another
bankable and critical success (tellingly, it was described by Larushka Ivan-
Zadeh as featuring an 'engaging signature ensemble [who] tackle bourgeois
problems with added global complications' [2017]). Klapisch was born on
4 September 1961, to Jewish parents, in Neuilly-sur Seine, a wealthy resi-
dential neighborhood in northwest Paris. He was a film studies student at the
prestigious Paris-III University, where he graduated with a thesis titled '*Le
nons-sens au cinéma, 6e sens du 7e art*' (based on a comparative reading of
Tex Avery cartoons and the films of Woody Allen and the Marx Brothers).
Frustrated at having twice failed the entrance exam to Paris's prestigious
film school Institut des Hautes Etudes Cinématographiques (IDHEC, now
known as La Fémis), Klapisch left France to study film at New York University in 1983. It seemed an opportune moment to leave. Klapisch has often

railed against 1980s film culture in France arguing that it was still being held prisoner by what he described as the dated, mind-numbing aesthetics of the New Wave. In America, he would later admit, 'there was more to life than [Jean-Luc] Godard' (Antoine 2005).[1] While there, he trained first as a camera operator, and then as a writer-director, making a series of eye-catching short films (*Glamour toujours*, *Un, deux, trois mambo*, *Jack le menteur* and *In Transit*[2]). It was a liberating experience for him professionally and personally. In an interview in 1997, he explained how the transatlantic trip stimulated his future style:

> [In America], I learned to be more concrete, not to use a symbol as the starting point of a screenplay, but rather to use an image that I like, and then to try to bring that image into the service of the script. [Americans] tackle everything more simply and less intellectually [than the French].
> (quoted in Kammoun-Carlet 1997)

This focus on concrete images, rapidity, simplicity and a refusal to over-intellectualize (in the same interview with Kammoun-Carlet, he termed his newfound approach 'the just do it' style) has become the hallmark of Klapisch's career. Returning to France, he began his apprenticeship in the film industry, assisting Leos Carax on *Mauvais sang/Bad Blood* (1986), directing his first short film, *Ce qui me meut* in 1989 (which would subsequently become the name of his production company) and making a documentary on the Kenya Massai warriors for cable television channel Canal Plus. In 1992, Klapisch made his first feature film, *Riens du tout/Little Nothings*. This story of a new CEO, charged with boosting employee morale at a failing Parisian department store, established the Klapisch touch and laid down a set of stylistic and thematic tenets that have recurred in most of his films since – a critique of modern management techniques imposed by the imperatives of globalization, the trope of the family, male and female interaction and (mis)communication, the vitality of youth culture, and the importance of setting. In *Little Nothings*, the '*Grandes Galeries*' store, with its twenty-four different characters, each with their own foibles and tics, serves as a microcosm for Paris itself, just as the 'Spanish Apartment' would reflect 'young Europe' a decade later. In an interview with the *Guardian* in 2003, shortly after the UK release of *The Spanish Apartment*, Klapisch declared his fondness for 'multicultural, melting-pot environment[s]'.

Families and communities in conflict is a recurring feature of his work. After *Little Nothings* came *Le Péril jeune/Good Old Daze*, followed by *Chacun cherche son chat/When the Cat's Away*, *Un air de famille/Family Resemblances* (1996), and *Peut-être/Perhaps* (1999). Each of these refine Klapisch's style, ricocheting between science-fiction and family drama and using

Paris not just as a collection of geographical or touristic markers but as a space onto which debates about post-1968 youth, multiculturalism, urban renewal and family dynamics could be mapped. *Good Old Daze* shares much of the same DNA as *The Spanish Apartment*. Set in the late 1970s, the film recounts the lives of four friends who left high school in Paris ten years earlier. Reuniting for the birth of the child of a fifth friend, Tomasi (Romain Duris), who has recently died, the young men reminisce about their time at school (drugs, girls, student demonstrations) and reflect on the passing of time, their uneasy transition into adulthood and their place in a post-1968 France. Using a soundtrack that included Janis Joplin, Jimi Hendrix and Pink Floyd, and dramatizing the familiar rites of passage trajectory of French youth, *Good Old Daze* struck a chord with audiences (nearly 650,000 tickets sold in France). It was successful partly because it offered an alternative to the heritage cinema and literary adaptations that French cinema had increasingly turned to; others saw it as an obvious mimicking of the American youth teen comedy. Audiences empathized with the onscreen depiction of Tomasi, Alain, Momo and others who had come of age in the 1970s, just as they themselves had. It remains Klapisch's favorite film; he has confessed that it is the 'worst directed' but most 'graceful' of his work (Anon. 2013).

Around this period, Klapisch became increasingly socially engaged as well. In 1994, he made the short films *Poisson Rouge* and *La Chambre* as part of his contribution to the French-based AIDS prevention campaign *3000 scénarios contre un virus* and in 1997 was a prominent signatory of the repressive anti-immigration Debré law (see Powrie 1999: 10–17). Such interventions form an important part of Klapisch's unpretentious intellectualism and non-didactic involvement in contemporary French politics and can be linked to the wider thematic concerns of his films, what Mireille Rosello calls 'self-conscious and self-referential attempts at participating in the construction of contemporary Europe' (2007: 17). The underlying themes of *When the Cat's Away* in 1996 also fed into Klapisch's interest in the downsides of social upheaval and modification. The film was a critique of urban renewal and gentrification in Paris and depicted the city as a space permanently in flux, whether architecturally, culturally or sociologically. These tensions between the old and the new, and the ramifications of these renewal projects on local community relationships, would reappear in *The Spanish Apartment* and offer evidence for the ongoing give and flex in Klapisch's films between the familiar and the new in both spatial and societal terms. Colin Nettelbeck distinguishes in Klapisch 'the hypersensitive combination of psychological intimacy and quirky sociology' (1999: 3). Nettelbeck is referring to *When the Cat's Away* here, but it is an apt summation of all of Klapisch's twelve films to date.

Several authorial elements recur in Klapisch's work. Jean Fallon has noted how 'he plays a small cameo role; in each film the wide-ranging soundtrack adds nuance to the themes; he employs many of the same actors to play very different characters in a variety of his films; he uses a dream or fantasy scene to comment on reality; he has a penchant for framing images through grids or breaking an image into many small pieces' (Fallon 2007: 202). As we shall see in Chapter 3, many of these motifs are deployed in *The Spanish Apartment*. We might also upscale Fallon's appraisal here by adding that the starting point for Klapisch's screenplays is frequently auto-biographical. As well as *The Spanish Apartment*, *When the Cat's Away* was based on his own recollections of a girlfriend who had left her cat with an elderly neighbor (who then subsequently lost the cat), while *Good Old Daze* is a nostalgic recreation of his own teenage years.[3] Recall too that Klapisch was named by Claude-Marie Trémois as one of French cinema's up-and-coming directors (Trémois 1997). Describing Klapisch as 'the most humanist, and the freest' (151) of the new generation of French filmmak-ers, Trémois noted how he mined the same thematic seam again and again: 'human relationships [. . .] how people perceive one another, how people get on, or don't get on, with one another, and how they communicate with each other' (151). Klapisch's films frequently explore this group dynamic, whether in a department store (*Little Nothings*), a high school (*Good Old Daze*), a Parisian neighborhood (*When the Cat's Away*) or six characters in a café (*Family Resemblances*). *The Spanish Apartment* once again depicts a 'family' under pressure, and subsequent Klapisch films have continued to do this, including *Paris* (2008), *Ma part du gâteau/My Piece of the Pie* (2011) and *Back to Burgundy* (2017). Most of these films feature young characters, either at the center or the periphery. *Paris* and *Family Resemblances* may focus on more mature characters who recall life's disappointments or roads not taken, but these characters still exhibit a childlike naivety.

Klapisch's films are not only freighted with a dynamic visual style, sureness of touch and sophisticated wordplay, but they are also humanist and heartfelt in their quasi-ethnographic depiction of human interactions. Much of his work is concerned with the overlapping of languages, cus-toms and cultural differences, and the inherent (often comic) tensions that inevitably occur when these factors bounce off each other in enclosed social spaces. Olivier Courson, the CEO of Canal Plus (the channel has copro-duced Klapisch's last five films) has applauded his 'extraordinary ability to tap into the vibes [and] the contemporary trends of a society' (quoted in Hopewell 2014). That is why *The Spanish Apartment* is more than just a film about the impact of the Erasmus program on a group of privileged white Europeans. Klapisch reveals the messiness of Xavier's relationships with the women in his life (his mother and Martine in Paris, Anne-Sophie,

Isabelle and Wendy in Barcelona) alongside Wendy's and Isabelle's own awkward romantic entanglements; he uses the muddled dynamics of the apartment to consider questions of language and identity (should one speak Catalan or Spanish in Barcelona; do Walloons speak Flemish or French?), the permanence of national stereotypes and the value of forging one's own future. These preoccupations are often embedded within the sonic fabric of Klapisch's films. He seeks to push his films beyond a narrow set of French artistic parameters, extending them beyond the strictly national towards the global. The soundtrack for *The Spanish Apartment* is a case in point here. Music has always been an important component of Klapisch's films, and he combines European electronica (Daft Punk) with Chopin and Charpentier, salsa, flamenco, Ali Farka Touré and Radiohead.

Thus, by the time preproduction began on *The Spanish Apartment*, Klapisch was admired for his fresh, spontaneous approach to filmmaking (he completed a number of assignments for French television in the late 1990s, to which he credits his rapid shooting style) and his skill at making films that combined both popular and auteur characteristics. His films were commercially popular (*Family Resemblances* sold 2.5 million tickets; *Perhaps* and *When the Cat's Away* around 700,000 each [Anon. 2018]), won awards (among many others, Klapisch has claimed a César for Best

Figure 2.1 Cédric Klapisch – watchful, incisive, contemporary

Image courtesy of Image courtesy of Photoshot

Screenplay for *Family Resemblances* and an International Critics Prize at the Berlin Festival for *When the Cat's Away*) and attracted some of French cinema's most accomplished actors (Fabrice Luchini, Juliette Binoche, Gilles Lelouche, Karin Viard). In this respect, Klapisch can be categorized as Moine's and Palmer's exemplary 'third-way' director, situated at the center of two contrasting force fields – at one end is the over-the-top comedy of exaggeration and mismatched couples; at the other lies the cerebral, hyper-intelligent, auteur-driven film. Alongside the likes of Jean-Pierre Jeunet and Agnès Jaoui in his home country, or further afield with Steven Soderbergh, Alfonso Cuarón and Michael Winterbottom, Klapisch serves as a model of a director who can flip from genre to genre while maintaining visual and thematic consistency.

Erasmus: 'becoming' European

> The opportunities are endless. The friends and memories last a lifetime.
>
> (Anon. 2017a)

As we mentioned briefly in the previous chapter, Klapisch's inspiration for the film stemmed from two earlier experiences: having been a foreign student in New York for two years in the mid-1980s and having visited his sister while she was an Erasmus student in Barcelona. In numerous interviews, Klapisch has talked extensively about the effect these formative influences had on him. First, Klapisch's cultural immersion at NYU made him not only conscious of his own specific French national identity but also much more acutely aware of the close, though often invisible, cultural ties that exist in Europe. *The Spanish Apartment* should likewise be viewed through this lens of cross-cultural understanding and the aspirations of the emerging generation of adults depicted in the film. By cutting the umbilical cord to France and moving to New York for an extended period, Klapisch anticipated the later journey made by Xavier and the other European students in *The Spanish Apartment*. Klapisch became the hero of his own *Bildungsroman*, using his time in America to stage his own personal and professional development. Second, Klapisch's own sister was an Erasmus student in Barcelona during the late 1980s, and he visited her in the apartment that she shared with four other foreign students. Simply by being there and watching the flatmates interact, Klapisch (2012) sensed the emergence of a new generation: 'They lived together and reinvented undogmatically a new way of life without realizing it. They were the image of Europe in full spontaneous and enthusiastic construction'.[4]

Named after the sixteenth-century Dutch humanist, philosopher and con-tinental traveler, the Erasmus program – The European Community Action Scheme for the Mobility of University Students – offers European university students the opportunity to study for a semester and up to a year abroad. Devised in part to reflect Erasmus, the man's own commitment to tolerance, the unity of European culture and passion for mobility, this shining example of 'officially sanctioned European connectivity' (Gott 2015: 195) was cre-ated in 1987 and has been in existence ever since. The Erasmus program has at its heart the goal of eliminating, or at least eliding, walled-off nationalism and xenophobia while at the same time encouraging young Europeans to reflect on their individual conceptions of nationhood and identity within the supranationalizing Europe of the twenty-first century. In 2014, the EU's 'Erasmus Impact Study' noted that around 25% of Erasmus students met their long-term partners while studying abroad, and over a million babies had been born as a result.[5] At the time of *The Spanish Apartment*'s release in 2002, around 115,000 European students spent a 'year abroad' through Erasmus, with around 19,000 of them choosing to study in the scheme's most popular destination, Spain. The most recent statistical breakdown of Eras-mus participation in 2013–2014 saw Spain as still the most popular destina-tion, hosting nearly 25,000 Erasmus students. Spain also, each year, sends the most students abroad with 37,000 students leaving for another country in 2013–2014 (France, Germany, Italy and the UK are second to fifth for student take-up).[6] By 2017, as the program celebrated its thirtieth birthday, Erasmus had benefitted 3.3 million exchange students all over Europe.[7]

The advantages for an Erasmus participant's post-university professional career are clear. Sixty percent of Erasmus students think that their trip was beneficial for their first job, thanks to newly acquired language skills and the development of less quantifiable skills such as tolerance, open-mindedness and teamwork. More and more universities across Europe now make an Erasmus-style study abroad experience compulsory. Erasmus has been much discussed by political scientists, educators, anthropologists and politi-cians. Stefan Wolff has termed young EU citizens the 'Erasmus generation', sowing the seeds for a future European identity and approach to government that will be more consensual and collaborative: 'Give it 15, 20 or 25 years, and Europe will be run by leaders with a completely different socializa-tion from those of today [. . .] there will be less national wrangling, less Brussels-bashing and more unity in EU policy making' (quoted in Bennhold 2005). By 2012, Erasmus students already represented 5% of all European graduates; Wolff's 'leaders', it is hoped, will be the likes of Xavier, Wendy, Isabelle and so on, whose experiences in Barcelona a decade earlier have instilled in them a sense of European civics, tolerance and global perspec-tive. A cultural exchange program as much as a student mobility initiative,

Erasmus offers what could be regarded as the ideal experience for young people in Europe: an opportunity to study and socialize in a foreign European city with other like-minded students from across the continent. But, as *The Spanish Apartment* makes clear, the 'study abroad' component of the Erasmus experience is not necessarily its most important aspect (Klapisch shows us only one scene in a lecture theater, Wendy refuses to go out to a nightclub because she needs to study, Tobias revises for a test, and that's about it).[8]

Papatsiba (2006) notes that while the acquisition of intercultural competence was never a key directive of the Erasmus program, it was clearly a hoped-for outcome by its founders. Embedded within these lofty aims is a utopian desire to forge a new generation of European citizens who are eager to 'internalize a "European consciousness"' (109). Multiple studies of student mobility and European identity building have generally come to the same conclusion: that those students who spend time abroad feel more European than those participants who do not study in a foreign country (King and Ruiz-Gelices 2003; Fligstein 2008; Van Mol 2013; Van Mol and Timmermann 2014). For instance, Kristine Mitchell (2015) has demonstrated that among British students, around 75% of participants who 'never' identified with Europe before Erasmus regarded themselves as Europeans on their return (339–40). King and Ruiz-Gelicies argue that students who spend a year abroad are more favorable towards future European integration, feel themselves as belonging to Europe and have more knowledge of European affairs (2003: 245), while van Mol (2013) suggests that the mixture of young adults on exchange programs would lead to greater European cohesion and the creation of a 'People's Europe'. For van Mol, 'European identity should not be regarded equally as identification with the EU and its institutions [but instead that] Europe can be divided into multiple Europes' (2013: 210).

All of these insights reinforce the positive impact of Erasmus on individual and collective identity and in turn bolster Klapisch's own view of the advantages of cultural exchange and mobility among European youth. As Verstraete notes, traveling around Europe and interacting with other Europeans is a vital way of 'making each identify not just with his or her own locality but with Europe as a whole' (2010: 41). A committed Europhile, Klapisch too has always spoken positively about Erasmus, extolling the virtues of its horizon-broadening outlook, and stressing the importance of youth to the rolling rejuvenation and sustainability of the European project. Erasmus is, he told Hervé, 'an extraordinary moment of life [. . .] it creates a new generation of minds' (2002a). Many of the film's comedic moments are autobiographical fragments straight out of Klapisch's own lived experiences, taken verbatim from his time visiting his sister in Barcelona or when he lived in New York – one flatmate eating at 7 p.m., the other at midnight; Wendy confusing the words 'fuck' and 'fac'; the subdivided refrigerator; and so on.

In terms of engaging with broader perspectives about European youth culture, *The Spanish Apartment* also reflects another key by-product of the Erasmus program – having fun. Surveys completed by returning Erasmus students frequently point to very high levels of satisfaction with the experience abroad (Krzaklewska and Krupnik 2007; Teichler 2002; Alfranseder, Fellinger and Taivere 2011). Ewa Krzaklewska (2013) has suggested that this high, often euphoric, level of satisfaction with the Erasmus experience can in part be explained by the fact that a story of 'being an Erasmus student' fits very well into contemporary discourses around youth and adulthood (2013: 79). For Krzaklewska and others, the Erasmus experience can be framed as part of a wider journey on the part of the individual student from adolescence to adulthood and is often a period of fun, exuberance and unrestrained hedonism before the inevitable transition back into a world of responsibility and thoughts of future employment. She notes that, in (auto) biographical terms, Erasmus is 'the 'fun' part [. . .] filled with joy, entertainment, parties, travelling and meeting new people' (2013: 80). Returning Erasmus students talk about this period as a deferring of adult responsibility, an abrogation of social norms and expectations and a willed retreat to an unrestrained social life, freedom, experimentation and spontaneity. *The Spanish Apartment* captures these feelings of youthful hedonism very successfully. We see the students in bars and nightclubs, dancing, smoking marijuana, making new friends, embracing new cultures, having casual sex and engaging in typical student/youth activities. Klapisch depicts a generation of privileged European youth who can travel, spend money, and unproblematically postpone the transition to adulthood.

The Spanish Apartment is perhaps best classified as a film about delayed adulthood and the willingness to remain in a liminal space between student and adult. The film, much like the ongoing evaluation of the Erasmus program itself, suggests that Erasmus is slowly changing the mind-sets of European youths and helping to forge new networks of friends, relatives and life partners – so far, so utopian. But as we shall see, Klapisch's cohort of receptive Erasmus students could hardly be regarded as representative of European youth at the start of the twenty-first century. We shall return to this problematic portrayal.

Raising *The Spanish Apartment*

Even if he did not know it at the time, for Klapisch, the collective experiences of his time in New York and his exposure to the dynamics of the Erasmus program lent themselves to a future film. Alongside these autobiographical fragments, *The Spanish Apartment* weaves a range of sociological, political and cultural intertexts within its coming-of-age generic credentials. One of the most important of these was the concept of a united Europe and France's place with an increasingly borderless, blended continent. Klapisch's aim for the film was 'to show that in becoming European, once becomes more French, more Spanish, more English' (quoted in Fallon 2007: 205). Thus *The Spanish Apartment* is a conscious attempt to collapse difference while at the same time strengthening the bonds of nationhood and citizenship in an increasingly globalized world of flows and exchanges. Klapisch shot the film in the late summer of 2001, but by the time of its release in France in June 2002, France had seen the far-right Front National candidate Jean-Marie Le Pen reach the second round of the presidential elections with 18% of the popular French vote. Le Pen campaigned on pulling France out of the EU and reintroducing the franc as national currency, a year earlier had condemned the Schengen, Maastricht and Amsterdam treaties as foundations for 'a supranational entity spelling the end of France' (Shields 2007: 283), and in 2004, while campaigning for the European elections, set out the case for the pernicious, federalizing impact of the EU and France's inevitable 'absorption into the Euro-globalist magma' (Shields 2007: 299). While we should not fall too easily into the reflectionist trap of film history here, what is undeniable is that *The Spanish Apartment* was released at a time when certain sections of France were articulating feelings of unease and uncertainty about what they saw as a steadily fragmenting European project (coincidentally, *Russian Dolls* was released in France seventeen days after the French strongly rejected the ratification of the proposed Constitution of the European Union).

When work on what was to be his next project, the noir thriller *Ni pour ni contre, bien au contraire/Not For, or Against (Quite the Contrary)*, was pushed back four months in early 2001, Klapisch quickly returned to his embryonic ideas about a group of Erasmus students living together he had developed a decade earlier and managed to secure financing from television channels France 2 and Canal Plus on the back of a ten-page treatment. He then spent time interviewing Erasmus students from different European countries, developing the outline of a script based on their memories and experiences. Klapisch and his long-time producer Bruno Lévy then gave themselves just sixteen weeks to write and shoot the film (in part because of the overlapping schedules of the main actors). This very tight timeframe obliged Klapisch to shoot digitally for the first time (Klapisch 2002b). Turning the slight treatment into a workable screenplay took two further weeks, followed by extensive improvisation and workshopping, especially in the scenes set in the apartment, to enable the actors to feel part of a shared community. Often, Klapisch would meet his actors at a particular location in Barcelona or Paris (a street, a bar, a restaurant) and encourage them to improvise the scene from a few key words or ideas.[9] This is typical of Klapisch's working methods – he is known to improvise a lot on set and (re)work new ideas and unintended, serendipitous character dynamics into the final film. The film has been aptly described as 'a kind of streaming reality broken up by momentary splashes of dreams, fantasies and memories' (Anon.). This experimental patchwork approach to story structure seems an apt fit for *The Spanish Apartment*, given that Xavier, through whose eyes we see the film, is a writer who is endlessly rewinding and rewriting his experiences of a particular event.

Stylistically too, the film's multiple deployment of visual patterns of assemblage, collage and cutting-and-pasting mirrors Klapisch's working style. It is worth noting too that the plot of *The Spanish Apartment* has often been described as 'inconsequential', 'slight' and 'thin'. Jacqueline Nacache has argued that the plots of many films that make up the 'Young French Cinema' movement – including those by Klapisch – tend to ignore the narrative determinism that typifies mainstream cinema. Instead, the audience 'is invited to enter hushed worlds on tiptoe, rather than follow a sequence of well-oiled events (2015: 191). While *The Spanish Apartment* is intimist, and at times spatially enclosed, one would hardly describe it as 'hushed'. Yet Nacache is correct to observe how these kinds of films resemble 'a sketch that only achieves a final form through the process of the mise-en-scène' (191). The genesis of the script for *The Spanish Apartment*, coupled with Klapisch's hyper-stylized visuals, suggests a filmmaking process that developed as it went along and found its final form in post-production and the editing suite.

Casting was done ad hoc, without a set shooting script. Klapisch cast his fictional alter ego Duris first and then spent time criss-crossing Europe with his three casting directors to find the other six members of the 'Spanish apartment', who, in his words, needed to 'epitomize' Germans, Italians, Spaniards, Danes and English. The actors workshopped skeleton sections of the script set in the apartment with Duris on hand to model the genial, easy interactions that would eventually make their way into the finished film.

Who's who?

Klapisch's quirky casting choices have always been a strong aspect of his films. In his review of *The Spanish Apartment*, Michel Guilloux noted how the director 'cherishes' his actors, which allows him to capture their fleeting gestures and interactions more easily (2002). The four principal French-speaking actors here are now established names in contemporary French cinema, and three have moved beyond their domestic film industries to

Table 2.1 Who's who?

Character	Actor	Nationality	Role	Personality traits
Xavier	Romain Duris	French	'Hero': leaves Paris to spend a year in Barcelona, ostensibly to improve his job prospects	Curious, frustrated, angry, adventurous, prone to jealousy and depression
Martine	Audrey Tautou	French	Xavier's Parisian girlfriend	Faintly shrewish, needy, gradually drifts apart from Xavier
Isabelle	Cécile de France	Belgian	Erasmus student, studies economics with Xavier, moves into the apartment midway through the film	Strong-willed, potential love interest for Xavier – then reveals she is a lesbian
Wendy	Kelly Reilly	English	Erasmus student in the apartment	Maternal, bossy, may or may not have feelings for Xavier
Soledad	Cristina Brondo	Spanish	Erasmus student in the apartment	Having a relationship with Lars, very underdeveloped character
Lars	Christian Pagh	Danish	Erasmus student in the apartment	Having a relationship with Soledad, also has a child and a partner, speaks fluent French
Alessandro	Federico d'Anna	Italian	Erasmus student in the apartment	Underdeveloped character: smokes a lot, hippyish
Tobias	Barnaby Metschurat	German	Erasmus student in the apartment	Wants 'good vibes' in the apartment, suffers at the hands of William

Character	Actor	Nationality	Role	Personality traits
William	Kevin Bishop	English	Wendy's brother, comes to visit	'Little Englander': drinks heavily, urinates in the street, casually racist, redeems himself at the end
Jean-Michel	Xavier de Guillebon	French	Ex-pat neurosurgeon	Faux-bourgeois, slightly arrogant
Anne-Sophie	Judith Godrèche	French	Jean-Michel's wife	Reserved, timid, *coincée* (uptight)

work on international projects. Romain Duris (b. 1974) started his career in Klapisch's *Good Old Daze* and has worked with the director six more times, up to *Chinese Puzzle*.[10] For Klapisch, it is Duris's 'way of not expressing himself [that is] very expressive' (Lucia 2009). Along the way, Duris has taken advantage of this blankness and ability to interiorize his emotions in a variety of versatile roles for auteur directors like Tony Gatlif (*Gadjo Dilo*, for which he was nominated for the César Award for Most Promising Actor), Christophe Honoré (*Dans Paris/Inside Paris*, 2006), Michel Gondry (*Mood Indigo*, 2013) and François Ozon (*Une Nouvelle amie/The New Girlfriend*, 2014). Many interviews with Duris, or reviews of his performances, refer to him as a '*Parisien branché*' (trendy Parisian), complete with distinctive, unruly hair, prominent cheekbones, and permanent five o'clock shadow. Cynthia Lucia (2009) has described the actor as 'an interesting mixture of experience and innocence, intelligence and naiveté, confidence and uncertainty', qualities which are on show in many of his films. Like Klapisch, Duris has shuttled between commercial, popular cinema and weightier, auteur-driven work. The ongoing partnership between the two men inevitably recalls that of director François Truffaut and actor Jean-Pierre Léaud and their 'Antoine Doinel' cycle, shot over twenty years between 1959 and 1979.[11]

   Duris's most critically acclaimed role to date is that of Thomas Seyr in Jacques Audiard's crime drama *De battre mon coeur s'est arrêté/The Beat That My Heart Skipped* (2005), a remake of James Toback's *Fingers* (1978). In his analysis of Duris's performance in that film, Douglas Morrey spots a number of Duris's repeated naturalistic gestures: the movement of Duris's eyebrows, his ironic smiles, a gaze that flits from left to right, eyeballs that won't stay still when he is observing someone. This is an agitated performance, notes Morrey: one of nervous tension mixed with spontaneity aided by Duris's ability 'to show the rapid passage of several emotions on his face' (2016: 201). Though trading in a far different genre, Duris exhibits similar gestures in *The Spanish Apartment*, *Russian Dolls* and *Chinese Puzzle*, such as the restless gaze and the nervous smile. Seyr and Xavier are also similar in another way: both are young men making the difficult transition from adolescence to adulthood.[12] Even though Xavier is twenty-five in *The Spanish Apartment* (and Duris was twenty-seven when shooting began), Klapisch and Duris endow him early on with several infantilizing features to accentuate his coming of age over the course of the film (haircut, clothing, a callow, vacant look, screaming at his mother). Some of Duris's performative touches are quite beautifully delivered, such as the scene when he unselfconsciously plays air guitar on his bed next to Isabelle and smiles vacantly, moving his head to the beat of the music. For an actor who is now the epitome of a certain kind of easy, masculine, sophisticated charm, his sheer dorkiness in this brief moment adds an extra layer to Xavier's maturation.[13]

By far the most famous actor in *The Spanish Apartment* was Audrey Tautou (b. 1976), who was cast as Martine shortly before the phenomenal success of her performance as Amélie, in *Le Fabuleux Destin d'Amélie Poulain/Amélie* (Jean-Pierre Jeunet, 2001). While French audiences were already familiar with Tautou after her breakthrough, and award-winning role, in Tonie Marshall's *Vénus beauté (institut)/Venus Beauty (Institute)* (1999), it was her performance as the eponymous heroine of Jeunet's film – a shy Parisian waitress who decides to commit random acts of kindness – that brought her global fame. The gamine face and 'child-woman' persona showcased in *Amélie* has been crucial to her enduring international appeal and has been much discussed and analyzed. Critics have observed how Tautou authenticates the social values of her time and presents an unthreatening form of young femininity (Vincendeau 2001; Vanderschelden 2007).[14] Since *The Spanish Apartment*, she has worked with auteurs (Alain Resnais, Stephen Frears, Anne Fontaine) and starred opposite Tom Hanks in *The Da Vinci Code* (Ron Howard, 2006).

Cécile de France (b. 1975) was a theater-trained Belgian actress who won the César Award for Most Promising Newcomer for her role as Isabelle.[15] De France has since emerged, like Duris and Tautou, as a performer skilled at cutting across multiple genres. In the few years after *The Spanish Apartment*, she played a psychopathic killer in *Haute Tension/High Tension* (2003), the female lead in a Hollywood version of *Around the World in 80 Days* (2004) and Gérard Depardieu's love interest in the romance *Quand j'étais chanteur/When I Was a Singer* (Xavier Giannoli, 2006). Kelly Reilly (b. 1977) had played only minor roles before *The Spanish Apartment*, but since, she has worked consistently in Hollywood (*Sherlock Holmes*

Figure 2.2 Romain Duris and Audrey Tautou: emerging adults, emerging stars
Image courtesy of Photofest

[Guy Ritchie, 2009], *Flight* [Robert Zemeckis, 2012]), in British film (*Mrs. Henderson Presents* [Stephen Frears, 2005], *Eden Lake* [James Watkins, 2008]) and television (the second season of *True Detective* [2015]). She won the Chopard Trophy as 'Female Revelation of the Year' at Cannes in 2005 as well as a César Best Supporting Actress nomination for reprising the role of Wendy in *Russian Dolls*. Judith Godrèche (b. 1972) was the most experienced of the cast, having made her debut in 1985 alongside Claudia Cardinale and Fanny Ardant in Nadine Trintignant's *L'été prochain/Next Summer*. Before working with Klapisch, she had acted for, among others, Benoît Jacquot, Olivier Assayas and Patrice Leconte and was familiar to international audiences for playing Leonardo diCaprio's love interest in *The Man in the Iron Mask* (Randall Wallace, 1998). The remaining main actors (Barnaby Metschurat, Cristina Brondo, Kevin Bishop, Federico d'Anna and Christian Pagh) have continued to work in film, television and theater in their native countries.

'Like a jewel in the sun': Barcelona as backdrop

'You will have fun', says Jean-Michel to Xavier at Barcelona airport. He is, of course, not at this point talking about the adulterous relationship Xavier is about to have with his new wife Anne-Sophie but rather referring to the sunny climate, nightlife and hedonistic pleasures on offer in Barcelona. According to Helio San Miguel and Lorenzo J. Torres Hortelano (2013), around 25% of all films made in Spain (around fifty per year) are shot in Barcelona. As well as a recurring setting for domestic filmmakers, international directors have also set films there (Whit Stillman's *Barcelona* [1994], Woody Allen's *Vicky Cristina Barcelona* [2008] and Alejandro González Iñárritu's *Biutiful* [2010]), drawn in part by Barcelona's striking urban landscape and its omnipresent avant-garde art and architecture.[16] Given the universality of the film's themes, Klapisch admitted he could have chosen to shoot in any number of European cities (London, Berlin, Copenhagen), but he already had a personal connection to Barcelona after visiting his sister there and also saw how the city's status as a multiethnic Mediterranean port and a diverse melting pot of coexisting hybrid identities (Spanish, Catalan, foreign student, etc.) could serve his wider thematic preoccupations:

> I knew the city and had fallen in love with its diversity. For many reasons, it is typical of Europe – because it is both very old with its historical sites and very modern with its incredible nightlife, and both very cosmopolitan but with its own strong Catalan identity. These paradoxes are what make Europe so complex and rich.
>
> (quoted in Anon. 2003)

When Klapisch visited his sister there, he noticed the slow cultural and urban revitalization that was taking place in the long aftermath of the regime of General Franco, who ruled Spain as a military dictatorship from 1939 to his death in 1979. At this time, Barcelona had also been chosen to host the 1992 Olympic Games (which kick-started a wave of urban gentrification and expansion the consequences of which Klapisch would later explore, in a French context, in *When the Cat's Away*). Culturally, things were changing. *La Movida Madrileña* (the Madrid 'scene') was an underground countercultural movement that flourished in the aftermath of Franco's death. After years of repression and conformity, the nation's cultural scene changed dramatically with the relaxation of censorship laws and church regulations. It championed youth and the breaking down of old cultural taboos and led to new modes of artistic expression in film, fashion, music, drugs, graffiti and urban nightlife.[17] It began in Madrid but quickly spread to cities like Vigo, Seville and Barcelona, where all-night parties and a wild, hedonistic lifestyle of the kind depicted in *The Spanish Apartment* flourished. Thus, Barcelona, for Klapisch, *is* Europe: receptive, rebellious, pluralistic, old and new, and in perpetual dialogue with itself.

Klapisch films Barcelona in the way that one might expect a foreign director to film a familiar city: he uses its monuments and markers as anchor points for those acquainted with Barcelona while at the same time

Figure 2.3 'Like a jewel in the sun': Barcelona, Gaudí and blue sky
Image courtesy of Alamy

averting his tourist gaze to focus on less well-known parts of the city.[18] Klapisch spotlights some of Barcelona's most enduring spaces to capture the itinerant joy of living in a foreign city. Over the course of *The Spanish Apartment*, characters visit, interact with each other and spend time alone in or at Plaça de Catalunya, Via Laietana, Plaça Reial, Carrer Escudellers Blancs, Parc Güell, Platja de la Barceloneta, Telefèric del Port, Rambla del Mar, the Museu d'Art Contemporani de Barcelona (MACBA) and the Sagrada Família, all of which unspool photogenically before us. This use of very specific geographical locations is quite different from the depiction of Paris in *When the Cat's Away* and *Paris*. In the former, Klapisch snubs the recognizable side of the city and focuses on a few streets in the eleventh *arrondissement*; in the latter, his attention is also drawn to more unfamiliar spaces in the capital (university buildings, market places, streets). For Klapisch, the locations in *When the Cat's Away* and *Paris* are fundamental to the stories he tells: 'the geography was related to the psychology of the people' (Lucia 2009).

In *The Spanish Apartment*, Klapisch also uses urban space in a precise way to tell us more about his characters (Xavier's identity shift is reflected in his ability to easily navigate the narrow backstreets; Anne-Sophie refers to Barcelona as being 'like the third world'; William urinates and vomits in its streets; and back in Paris, Xavier wanders tearfully through Montmartre, a place 'where only the tourists go'). In the pre-departure and post-return scenes, the French capital is construed as muted, conformist and bland. The Bercy ministry is faceless; Xavier's clothes are dark and ill fitting; colleagues discuss red and blue folders while drinking one-euro machine coffee. The moment Xavier steps off the bus in Barcelona, his attitude alters, and so too, it seems, does his response to external stimuli. The climate is responsible for Xavier's newly discovered candor. He writes to Martine at the beach, where it is hot and sunny and the sky is azure blue. When Xavier seduces Anne-Sophie after Isabelle's 'lesson', they return to her flat to make love. As they embrace, Klapisch films the couple standing in front of a window with Barcelona's streets and buildings in the background reflected onto their faces. The city, Klapisch suggests, is not just the site of Xavier's new sexual adventures, but it is also complicit in the adultery: a safe screen onto which Xavier and Anne-Sophie's fantasies (his: sexual abandon; hers: a loss of inhibition and reserve) can be projected.

Xavier's coming of age is also coded in the hyper-saturated color scheme. Reds, yellows, greens and blues saturate the screen. These great globs of primary colors offer a luminous alternative to Xavier's humdrum life in Paris. For the exterior shots, Klapisch and cinematographer Dominique Colin used a Sony HD24p high-definition digital camera, which gives Barcelona

Figure 2.4 Xavier and Anne-Sophie consummate their affair

Image courtesy of Alamy

an ultra-sharp focus and allows the texture and contours of its celebrated architecture to gleam.[19] Klapisch has long recognized a debt to the American street photographer Alex Webb, whose work is striking for the complex interplay among composition, color and framing and whose recurring theme is the ethnographic exploration of cultures far removed from his own, especially 'the notion of multiple cultures living side by side' (Coop 2017). Webb aspires to serendipitously capture 'real moments', often shooting in the Caribbean and Latin America – two places where intense and vibrant color are intrinsic aspects of the visual fabric. Several of Colin's tableaux-like shots of Barcelona, such as Xavier at the beach on his phone, atop the Sagrada Família and crossing the Plaça Reial, recall Webb's framing and use of color. Klapisch has commented that urban life is 'heterogeneous, plural, non-linear, accidental', and yet his films, like Webb's own photography, 'must rearrange and frame things, find their geometry and bring order' (da Cunha 2013). Colin's cinematography in *The Spanish Apartment* seeks a balance between these two impulses – the documentary 'thereness' of Barcelona vis-à-vis its aestheticized, hyper-real rendition.[20]

Much of the striking architecture showcased in *The Spanish Apartment* was designed by Antonin Gaudí, the great practitioner of Catalan Modernism. Gaudí's constructions often used nature as their starting points and were adorned with brightly colored mosaic tiles. Curves, twists, plant motifs, and asymmetrical shells and spirals recur in his work (the nave of the Sagrada Família, for example, resembles a tree rising to the roof); for the art critic Robert Hughes, Gaudí created an 'architecture of ecstasy' [2015: 241]). Gaudí's Parc Güell, with its mosaicked, twisting balconies and pavilions, is the backdrop for Xavier and Anne-Sophie's first steps towards their affair. His most famous work is the Sagrada Família basilica and church (it is Barcelona's most visited tourist attraction, with over 3 million visitors annually and is the city's defining exportable image). Multiple directors have used the Sagrada Família as the city's dominant spatial emblem, most notably Michelangelo Antonioni in *The Passenger* (1975). It appears inevitably in *The Spanish Apartment* too. Xavier and Anne-Sophie, during one of their afternoon walks around the city, reach the top of the tower; Anne-Sophie faints, but we never find out why. Exhaustion? Vertigo? Guilt at the prospect of cheating on her husband? Exhilarated at the extent of Gaudí's imagination? In typical Klapisch fashion, not everything is revealed or explained, and the audience is left to guess. For Lucy Fischer, what is especially noteworthy about films set in Barcelona 'is not simply how they plant Gaudí's monuments with in their fictional worlds, making his edifices the "co-stars" of their dramas, but how [. . .] their narratives invoke themes that are aesthetically embedded in Gaudí's work' (Fischer 2017: 122). For Fischer, such themes include impossible love, identity crises, sexual confusion and fantasy – all of which bubble away to a greater or lesser extent throughout *The Spanish Apartment*.

Spanish Apartments, Pot Lucks and Europuddings: which title?

Our title is *L'Auberge espagnole*. Or is it? Its literal translation from French to English is *The Spanish Apartment*. This is the title given the film for distribution and exhibition in the United States. In Canada it was known as *Pot Luck*, in Germany *Barcelona For A Year* and in Spain *Una casa de locos* (a madhouse), laying the emphasis here on the tensions of *convivencia* (house sharing, cohabitation). For a time in the UK, it was to be called *Euro Pudding*.[21] From the moment Klapisch visited his sister's apartment in Barcelona, he knew that his future film would be called *L'Auberge espagnole*. Moreover, Xavier himself describes the apartment he shares as an '*auberge espagnole* in the literal sense'. But '*auberge espagnole*' is also a cultural pun. In French, it has a figurative expression: as a messy situation to which everyone must contribute something in order to make it what it is; in other words 'you will get from it as much as you put in'. It refers to the practice in Spanish inns of the nineteenth century that did not have restaurants, so each traveler brought food with them, which was cooked in the inn and then distributed to the other guests. Similarly, 'pot luck' is a derivation of 'potlatch', the Native American custom of a communal meal where each guest would bring his or her own food.

While *The Spanish Apartment* contains its fair share of scenes of cultural conflict, the broader historical notions of community spirit, sharing and making do implicit in the French title are woven into the texture of the film. Xavier uses the examples of the apartment's communal refrigerator and telephone to illustrate the meaning of '*auberge espagnole*' to the audience: in the fridge, each shelf is subdivided and labeled. Cue a scene where Soledad incorrectly puts a carton of orange juice on Lars's shelf and he tells her to move it. The phone has a multilingual sign next to it to allow the person taking the call to communicate (albeit very basically) to the person making the call (which leads to Wendy's confusion when she speaks to Xavier's mother). These *faux pas* aside, the 'Spanish apartment' functions smoothly. Klapisch reinforces the sustainability of communal sharing further through the motif of cooking (the Italian teaches the flatmates to make pasta, the French how to make *gratin dauphinois*). As we shall see in the next chapter, the figurative term '*auberge espagnole*' illustrates Klapisch's own positive stance on intercultural understanding, dialogue and diversity but also reinforces the core sociological and cultural imperatives that underpin the Erasmus program, namely, the establishment of strong, temporary, bonds among young people from across Europe who each bring with them differing cultural, linguistic and emotional outlooks into the melting pot of the 'shared house'.

Release and reception: 'a European version of *Friends*'

The Spanish Apartment was released first in France in June 2002, where it became the fifteenth-highest grossing film of the year with highly respectable ticket sales of nearly 3 million and box office receipts of well over US$15 million.[22] It was also the fourth-highest grossing French film of that year (behind *Astérix et Obélix: Mission Cléopâtre/Asterix and Obelix: Mission Cleopatra* [dir. Alain Chabat], *8 femmes/8 Women* [dir. François Ozon] and *Le Boulet/Dead Weight* [dir. Alain Berbérian and Frédéric Forestier]). The statistical breakdown of admissions in those European territories represented by characters in the film also reinforces *The Spanish Apartment*'s popular appeal beyond the *hexagone*: Germany (363,000), Spain (304,000), Italy (512,000), Belgium (165,000) and the United States (646,000). It also won the Audience Award at the 2002 Karlovy Vary International Film Festival.

Most reviews and critical articles of *The Spanish Apartment* in France were upbeat, with many responding very positively to Klapisch's new offering after the lukewarm reception of his previous film, *Perhaps*. Some focused on the stylized depiction of Barcelona, others on the chaotic apartment arrangement as a metaphor for the ongoing wider process of European integration, and others on Klapisch's breezy directorial approach and humor-flecked screenplay. Several mainstream critics commented on *The Spanish Apartment*'s innovative narrative structure and its reliance on short, often surreal '*saynètes*' (sketches) to explore wider themes of integration, harmony and cross-cultural understanding. A favored adjective was 'refreshing'. For Jean-Paul Grasset (2002), the film's humor was 'occasionally overwhelming', but the overall effect was 'intelligent and sensitive'. A certain A. C. at *Les Echos* (2002) appreciated 'the gags, the laughter, the tenderness, and the humor' and the 'year-long initiation into love, liberty and Europe', while E. L. at *L'Express* (2002) noted that even though it was far too long, its nostalgia and warmth were welcomed. Amélie Dubois in *Les Inrockuptibles* likened Xavier to the eponymous hero of Voltaire's *Candide* heading off to Barcelona in a harmless rite of passage. *France-Soir* called it 'sparkling', admiring the way Klapisch's style mirrored Xavier's own personality: 'sometimes hesitant, sometimes passionate, sometimes zestfully, sometimes in turmoil' (Mereu-Boulch 2002b). Michel Guilloux (2002) at *L'Humanité* described the film as 'European Paella', drawing a direct link between Klapisch's work and *American Pie 1* and *2*. The French version, however, was 'kinder' and 'nicer' and avoided the traps of more recent gross-out and sex-obsessed American comedies.

Even the more tepid reviews were, on balance, broadly in favor of *The Spanish Apartment*. Several criticized the 'patchwork' nature of the film, arguing that there was no overarching narrative stitching everything together. Matthieu Darras in *Positif* (2002) called it 'a partial failure' (117), forever 'hammering home' its central message that we are all composed of multiple identities. Yet these reviews went on to argue that this turn away from a stable, settled narrative structure was a deliberate decision on Klapisch's part to focus instead on a series of fractured vignettes to better illustrate his vision of the European melting pot. Vincent Malausa (2002) called the apartment 'a great anarchic laboratory' and the goings-on in there 'a colourful baroque theatre' (86). Jean-Claude Loiseau (2002) concluded his glowing review of the film by in fact praising this *'dilettantisme narratif'* (narrative superficiality) as a way of reinforcing the key theme not just of *The Spanish Apartment* but of Klapisch's entire body of work up to that point: 'la vie en vrac [. . .] ces moments où il ne se passe presque rien mais où on dit presque tout' (*'life as a mess [. . .] those moments when hardly anything happens but when virtually everything is said'*).

There were some strongly dissenting voices. Samuel Blumenfeld (2002) in *Le Monde* was highly critical, calling it clichéd and simplistic. It resembled a 'version of "Loft Story" [the French equivalent of the TV reality show *Big Brother* that premiered in France in April 2001] sponsored by the EU'; it was 'naïve', 'moralistic' and 'caricatured'. Fabrice Plisken in *Le Nouvel Observateur* (2002) denounced the film as an advertisement for the EU (not least because all of the students appeared to have 'white teeth and anatomically correct bodies'). This charge of unrepresentative casting was also a criticism leveled by Edward Ousselin, whose extended reading of the film reproached Klapisch for only including one black character, despite the fact that both Paris and Barcelona were vast multiethnic, multiracial cities. Ousselin's conclusion was that the film was more widely indicative of French cinema's continual struggle with the contemporary realities of ethnic diversity (2009: 756). Plisken, like Blumenfeld, also drew unfavorable comparisons with 'Loft Story' and concluded that the endless decorum and pleasantry of Klapisch's version of student life made one nostalgic for the unadulterated vulgarity of *American Pie*.

Beyond France, international critics welcomed the film. On the review aggregator website 'Rotten Tomatoes', the film currently (April 2018) has an approval rating of 77%, based on 91 reviews, with an average rating of 6.5/10.[23] The following US examples reflect the broadly positive acknowledgement of Klapisch's work: 'Imagine the American students in

"The Real Cancun" [a US reality film following sixteen students on spring break] as if they were literate, cosmopolitan and not substance abusers, and you've got it' (Ebert 2003); 'Yet another example of [. . .] Klapisch's way of finding fresh new insights within the most mundane of circumstances'; 'a Euro pajama party' (Denby 2003); 'Klapisch demonstrates an understanding for the way young people caught between the demands of adulthood and their lingering adolescence behave' (Rodriguez 2003).

Surprisingly, in the UK, audience figures were very disappointing $(21,000)^{24}$ and the critical reception decidedly cool. Ben Walters's lukewarm review in *Sight and Sound* was symptomatic of the British consensus. While he (reluctantly) admired the 'the postcard-friendly compositions, meandering plot and expensive, eccentric castlist', he quickly tired of the 'random episodes piling up towards the end underpinned by very little sense of purpose' (Walters 2003: 55). Similarly, for *The Guardian*, it was 'never dull exactly, but shallow and naïve' (Bradshaw 2003), and for the BBC, it felt 'underpowered' and 'only modestly entertaining' (Dawson 2003). Several online reviews in the UK compared *The Spanish Apartment* unfavorably to both *This Life* (1996–1997; 2007), a BBC drama series that charted the messy lives and loves of five twenty-something law graduates sharing a house in London, and *Friends* (1994–2004), the American NBC sitcom that followed six 'emerging adult' friends living the same apartment block in New York. This ambivalent response was replicated in Australia. *The Spanish Apartment* won an audience award at the Brisbane International Film Festival and both the most popular film and the jury's Prix UIP award for best European film at the Sydney Film Festival. Paul Byrnes (2003) in the *Sydney Morning Herald* lauded Klapisch's 'close and affectionate observation' of the characters, labeling him 'a generous chronicler of life, satirical but not mean'. Lawrie Zion (2003), in a move similar to several reviews in France, applauded Klapisch for making a film 'that is so inviting that it could be used as propaganda to promote the very idea of European unity'. On the other hand, Adrian Danks (2003) in *Senses of Cinema* was no fan, calling it a 'rarely funny sub-*Amélie*' attended by an audience who 'tried extremely hard to have a good time'.

Ideological readings of *The Spanish Apartment* have been similarly extremely eclectic. Most of them make reference to Xavier's *Bildungsroman* trajectory, the concept of individual and collective identity and multiculturalism in Barcelona. In addition, it has been read as reinforcing privileged linguistic and cultural exchange among European youths (Blum-Reid 2009); a laboratory experiment to test ideas of intercultural identity and sensitivity (Derakhshanim and Zachman 2005); a plea to bolster the value of European cultural diversity (Béguin 2004); a sanitized, de-historicized deception of Barcelona (Ezra and Sánchez 2005); a version of Sartrean existentialism (Boulé 2011); a critique of exchange value and Euronorma-tivity (McCaffrey and Pratt 2011); emblematic of the unfinished nature of Europe (Rosello 2007); extolling the benefits of multilingualism (Warren 2008); abetting the normalization of the Erasmus program (Ousselin 2009); and reflecting the transnational global economies of exchange, whether that be people, cultures or languages (Amago 2007).

Of particular note in terms of Xavier's coming of age and his emerging adult status are the contrasting approaches to the film taken by Mireille Rosello, Mana Derakhshani and Jennifer A. Zachman, and Jean-Pierre Boulé. Rosello proposes the notion of a 'chaotic border' to analyze in more detail the role of language, group dynamics and the European project in both *The Spanish Apartment* and *Russian Dolls*. She moves away from the common reading of the film as an allegorical reconstruction of Europe to suggest instead that *The Spanish Apartment* is an example 'of how self-contained episodes, with their open-ended lessons, their emphasis on messi-ness [and] 'to be continued' quality to them are the best possible way of representing the construction of a twenty-first century European "mess" ' (Rosello 2007: 30). Derakhshani and Zachman pay attention to Barcelona's artistic relevance as the home not just of Gaudí but also of the painters Salvador Dali and Pablo Picasso. They see reflected in the trio's output aspects of Xavier's emerging identity – Gaudí's fluid, curved style forms the backdrop for Xavier's increasingly erotic encounters with Anne-Sophie; Picasso's cubist style is mapped onto the film's fragmentary narrative, split screens, and choppy montage; and Dali's surrealism is explicitly visualized in Xavier's dream sequence, in which his entire identity – as well as his native language – seems to break down entirely.[25]

For Derakhshani and Zachman, *The Spanish Apartment* also offers 'a met-onymic representation of national and intercultural identities of the "new" Europe' that can be traced through the protagonist Xavier's 'evolution as a character and an interculturally sensitive narrator' (129). Xavier's devel-opment as an individual takes place in a city that epitomizes Catalonia's regional and linguistic heterogeneity and also reflects Europe's increasing cultural hybridity. Thus, Barcelona represents the possibilities of a 'multi-ethnic, multilingual, multicultural Europe' (132). Boulé takes a very dif-ferent tack, detecting in both *The Spanish Apartment* and *Russian Dolls* explicit references to Jean-Paul Sartre's existentialism and in particular his novel *La Nausée/Nausea* (1938). So, Xavier is not 'free' in the Sartrean sense throughout *The Spanish Apartment* because he is not exercising his freedom (to commit to Martine, to not follow the career path of his father, to become a writer), and his visions of Erasmus as he falls into a depression in Barcelona are at first, like Roquentin's bad dreams in *Nausea*, the realization that he is afraid of existence but then the first step towards absolute freedom and a lucid self-actualization. For Boulé, over the course of *The Spanish Apartment* and *Russian Dolls*, Xavier has 'discovered his freedom, rejected the values of the bourgeoisie, examined his authenticity in writing, experience nausea, clarified the roles of the past, present and future in existentialist terms, experienced the Other in a positive way, showed that Humanism as an absolute doctrine is to be condemned but that humans are at the heart of our daily experience, and committed himself freely by formulating a project' (171). It is now time to turn to the film and focus in more detail on its visual style and narrative structure, its wider thematic resonances and its engagement with European youth.

Notes

1 In 1996, Klapisch had written an open letter to the French cultural magazine *Les Inrockuptibles* criticizing the New Wave as 'not being new anymore'.
2 *In Transit* featured an appearance by future American independent director Todd Solondz.
3 In 2014, Klapisch exhibited at Galerie Cinéma in Paris a series of photographs of Paris and New York he took while on preproduction for *Chinese Puzzle*. The gallery's press release stated that the photographs serve as a 'visual logbook' for Klapisch, inspiring ideas for his screenplays.
4 The transformative potential of the Erasmus scheme has also been endorsed by the Italian novelist and scholar Umberto Eco: 'I call it a sexual revolution: a young Catalan man meets a Flemish girl – they fall in love, they get married and they become European, as do their children. The Erasmus idea should be compulsory – not just for students, but also for taxi drivers, plumbers and other workers' (quoted in Riotta 2012).
5 Chris Green concluded in *The Independent* that 'young people searching for the partner of their dreams could do a lot worse than enrolling in the European Union's educational exchange programme' (2014).
6 *The Spanish Apartment* is set before the 2004 enlargement of the European Union, the largest single expansion of the EU to date, which saw the accession of Cyprus, the Czech Republic, Estonia, Hungary, Latvia, Lithuania, Malta, Poland, Slovakia and Slovenia. Today, European students may travel to and from these additional countries.
7 In 1987, 3,244 students enrolled in the scheme. In 2014, that number had reached 272,497. See 'Erasmus: Facts, Figures and Trends' (European Commission, 2015).
8 This lack of focus on Erasmus as an actual educational exchange is part of an ongoing discourse about the relevance and function of the scheme. For many critics, Erasmus has little to do with studying and engaging with local students/citizens. Instead it has become 'an EU-subsidized party in a foreign country'. See Viktor Gronne and Dalia Miklaseviciute (2014).
9 Tautou in particular found this fragmented process frustrating: 'in the screenplay, the only thing that was written about her character for this particular scene, was "she hates the world and the world hates her"' (Klapisch 2017).
10 While he was an art student in Paris, Duris was spotted in the street by a casting director.

11 The cycle comprises of four feature films – *Les 400 coups/The 400 Blows, Baisers volés/Stolen Kisses* (1968), *Domicile conjugal/Bed and Board* (1970) and *L'amour en fuite/Love on the Run* (1979) – and the 1962 short *Antoine and Colette*. Many of the interviews with Klapisch and the reviews of *The Spanish Apartment* included in the bibliography explicitly reference the Truffaut-Léaud connection. Stephen Holden (2006) in the *New York Times* called Klapisch 'Truffaut Lite'.

12 Rouyer and Vassé (2005) note that many of Duris's subsequent film roles after *Good Old Daze* emphasize his youthfulness and dramatize his (often fraught) transition to manhood.

13 When Catherine Shoard (2010) interviewed Duris, she was struck by Duris's 'completely transformative smile, capable of changing his face in the flick of a lip: from sexy to silly, brooding to buffoonish'.

14 The DVD cover for the UK and US release of *The Spanish Apartment* misleadingly positions Audrey Tautou as the star of the film (her face is at the center), despite her relatively minor role. *Amélie* was released while *The Spanish Apartment* was being shot.

15 She won a second César, this time for Best Supporting Actress, for *Russian Dolls* (2005).

16 The hospital Xavier visits to see Jean-Michel for his MRI scan is the Hospital del Mar. The same hospital also appeared in Pedro Almodóvar's *Todo sobre mi madre/All about My Mother* (1999), one of the very few of Almodóvar's films set in Barcelona.

17 Pedro Almodóvar's film *Pepi, Luci, Bom y otras chicas del montón/Pepi, Luci, Bom* (1980) captures this sense of cultural and sexual freedom of '*la Movida*'.

18 Klapisch will do the same with St. Petersburg and London in *Russian Dolls* and New York in *Chinese Puzzle*.

19 Shooting digitally also allowed Klapisch to use natural lighting. The scene in the apartment when there is a power cut and the flatmates search for the fuse box was entirely lit by a single cigarette lighter.

20 Colin returned as cinematographer for *Russian Dolls*. The DoP on *Chinese Puzzle* was Natasha Braier.

21 The term 'Euro Pudding' has a very specific meaning in English – it refers to bland European cinematic coproductions often conceived simply to take advantage of cross-border funding or subsidies and often lacking any sense of coherent identity or artistic purpose. In fact, Klapisch suggested to his UK distributors that the English-language title be *Euro Pudding*. Unaware of its pejorative connotations, he was eventually persuaded to release it as *Pot Luck*. For more on the concept of the 'Euro Pudding', see Liz (2015).

22 For a full breakdown of the top-grossing films in France in 2002, go to: www.boxofficemojo.com/intl/france/yearly/?yr=2002&p=.htm.

23 The site's critical consensus states: 'This multicultural comedy captures the chaos and excitement of being young'. Refer to: www.rottentomatoes.com/m/lauberge_espagnole/, accessed 17 June 2017. All subsequent references to US reviews of *The Spanish Apartment* are taken from the site.

24 Compare this figure to, say, *Hate* (45,000 in 1995/6), *When the Cat's Away* (45,000 in 1996/7) and *Amélie* (over 1 million in 2001).

25 In a 1997 interview, Klapisch praised the artists Alberto Giacometti, Nicolas de Staël and Giorgio Morandi for their ability to flit between the abstract and the symbolic (Kammoun-Carlet 1997).

3   *Bildungsroman* in Barcelona
Reading *The Spanish Apartment*

To be away from home and yet to feel oneself everywhere at home; to see the world, to be at the centre of the world, and yet to remain hidden from the world.

> (Charles Baudelaire, 'The Painter of Modern Life', 1863)

In heaven, all the policemen are British, all of the lovers are Italian, all of the chefs are French, all of the cars are German, and the whole thing is run by the Swiss.

In hell, all of the policemen are German, all of the lovers are Swiss, all of the chefs are British, all of the cars are French, and the whole thing is run by the Italians.

> (traditional joke)

The Spanish Apartment is divided into three distinct parts: going to Barcelona, living in Barcelona, and leaving Barcelona. We watch, and are guided through each stage by, Xavier. It is through his eyes and his voiceover that we gain an understanding of the complex trials of moving from the city where he has grown up to another where he finds himself unmoored and free-floating. In keeping with the narrative prerequisites of the *Bildungsroman*, Xavier makes new friends, takes new lovers, and learns life lessons about cultural identity, otherness and camaraderie. Along the way, Klapisch incorporates various editing styles, narrative devices, linguistic challenges and debates about identity and multiculturalism into Xavier's coming-of-age tale.

'This is how it starts': Klapisch's style

A black screen – then the name of Klapisch's production company '*Ce qui me meut*' appears in white.[1] Guillaume Dutrieux's trumpet wails. A man sits naked at a desk, working on his computer, an iMac G3. On his wall in front of him are a signed, red T-shirt with a large logo of a black bull, photographs and newspaper clippings. He yawns loudly, slowly. The trumpet becomes more plaintive, more muted. The screen fades to black. The trumpet sounds again. Black text written on turquoise oblong blocks appears. More oblong blocks appear, with two of them bearing the name, written in lowercase: romain duris. Another block contains the French tricolor flag. The music changes. It's no longer a trumpet but a singer in Spanish. We cut back to the man's room. He leans into his computer. A 9 × 8 grid of rectangles is overlaid onto the image. More names appear (judith godrèche, audrey tautou) and more flags. We cut to the man's fingers, typing in close-up. The music shifts once more, this time to a death-metal song, played with a high reverb. The overhead shot of the fingers then cuts to a shot of beachside boardwalk, with the same man we see at the desk now sitting in the foreground, flanked by palm trees, looking out towards a sapphire sea. The rhythm becomes more insistent. Embedded haphazardly within seventy-two rectangles, the name of each new actor is credited along with the flag of the country where their character is from: Belgium, Denmark, Germany, Spain, Britain. We cut back to the man. He's left the beach, and in a medium-long shot, we now see him holding a woman close to him. Another cut, this time to six young people sat around a table, looking directly at the camera. The images are now coming thick and fast: the man lies horizontally and enters a MRI chamber, documentary inserts of a crowd of people building a human tower, four young people prone on a couch, back to the keyboard with the hands typing more frantically, two young men seen in profile arguing, slowed-down footage of a young woman dancing, the same slowed-down dancing shot of another young man shown three different times within the rectangular grid, each time fragmented, as if missing parts of his body, the same technique used in the next cut, this time to the man and another woman. And then, finally we see the title: *l'auberge espagnole*, its letters repeated, laid on top of one another, in various font sizes, eventually coming into focus. Part one of the title sequence is over. Cast and title are clarified. We continue to the crew and return to some of the images introduced earlier: a close-up of the man in the MRI, a couple on a bicycle, the dancing woman's eyes in extreme close-up, the man kissing one woman and dancing with another, a group looking into a room from behind an ajar door, and then the sound, imperceptibly at first, but then louder and louder, of a plane taking off.

This credit sequence for *The Spanish Apartment* was created, as he has done for all of Klapisch's films bar *Family Resemblances*, by the French designer Eric Brocherie. It immediately establishes the film's visual and sonic palette. The slabs of color and sound, the fragmented, tessellated perspectives, the grid-like aesthetics, and the supple play with memory are all embedded within these opening two minutes. Retrospectively, of course, we learn that 'the man' is Xavier Rousseau, our main protagonist and narrator. The first shot of Xavier naked at his desk visualizes his first steps at writing his novel (to be called '*L'auberge espagnole*'), and the images shown in the credit sequence are Xavier's own memories of his time in Barcelona – the people he met, the places he visited, the music he listened to. The images he sees (as do we) are sometimes static, like photographs, and sometimes in motion, as if Xavier is replaying in his head scraps of a previous life. Klapisch has spoken of the importance of these Brocherie-designed credit sequences as a means of taking the viewer hostage and allowing them to better 'live' the start of the film both aesthetically and narratively. This is clearly the case here. A dazzling tour de force, the ninety-second sequence showcases Klapisch's visual brio and allegorizes the film's engagement with identity and cultural exchange. It is exuberant, colorful, innovative and fresh. By progressively superimposing the names of his cast over a cubist-style background of ever-changing oblongs, Klapisch lays out the film's multilingual and multicultural approach. The Latino-inflected song (composed by French composer and DJ Loïc Dury/aka Kouz-1) that plays over the credits primes us for the film's cosmopolitan, hybridized status. The opening also deploys a series of flash-forwards that project future characters, events and interactions and anticipate the fragmentary, elliptical splintering and (re)forming of identity that will occur to Xavier over the course of the film.

From the off, Klapisch flourishes his stylish credentials. John Hopewell defined what he regarded as the Klapisch 'touch' to the director himself in a 2014 interview:

> You really work hard for your money, try to entertain visually, whatever's going on in the plot. Your shots rarely hang around too long, often contrast visually, and can be semi-long shots with the characters

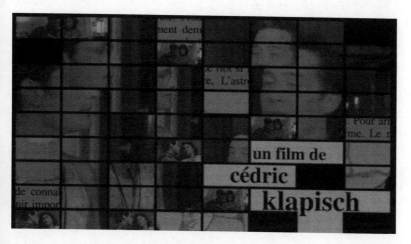

Figure 3.1 Visual style: grids and frames

in the middle of the scene allowing for multiple visual details in the foreground.

Several of these aspects are on display in *The Spanish Apartment*, whether in the inventiveness of the mise-en-scène (the aforementioned credit sequence, Xavier's first steps in Barcelona) or the staccato-like scenes in the apartment where it seems that Klapisch eavesdrops for a moment and then moves onto the next room or conversation. As we have already noted, Klapisch's decision to shoot in high-definition video enables him to be more inventive and spontaneous, capturing images quickly. The dazzling ingenuity of these opening moments will be reengineered throughout the rest of the film, and its two sequels: *Russian Dolls* (2005) and *Chinese Puzzle* (2013). In an interview in 2009, Klapisch admitted that he pivots between two opposing film tendencies: 'I like to stylize things and I like documentary shooting [. . .] I think it's fake to go in one direction only' (Lucia 2009). Across his career, he has combined these two aesthetic inclinations, folding stylization and artifice into reality and documentary.

There are numerous instances in *The Spanish Apartment* where Klapisch's inventive visual style is used to bolster a specific narrative concern or thematic impulse. For instance, he adds surreal gimmicks like the clicking sounds of stiletto heels and fast-motion footage as characters walk from point A to point B or the cutting of the frame into fragments. Such visual tropes serve to encourage a sense of simultaneity, whereby action happening in two different places at the same time seems, via cross-cutting editing, to be happening simultaneously (Alistair's arrival in Barcelona being the most obvious example). Klapisch calls such techniques 'quick but continuous' (Lucia 2009); it is an apt description of several scenes in *The Spanish Apartment*, such as the languid, casual walk down a Barcelona street by Xavier and Isabelle, reminiscent in its way of a similar scene between Jean-Paul Belmondo and Jean Seberg in Jean-Luc Godard's *A bout de souffle/ Breathless* (1960) in which two characters just talk, surrounded by noise, and cars and passersby, or the emergence of the flatmates from a nightclub to the pulsating arpeggios of Daft Punk's 'Aerodynamic' (2001) that Klapisch overlays with two slightly altered images to better capture their drunken, euphoric state.

Getting away from things

> My life's always been such a mess. Complicated, pathetic, untidy, completely chaotic. Life seems simple for everyone else.
>
> (Xavier)

Traditionally, in a *Bildungsroman*, the central protagonist will recount the experiences of their youth and/or young adulthood while attempting to make sense of the world, discover their place in that world, bear witness to events both important and trivial and come to terms with their identity, sexuality, beliefs and worldviews. While a novel can take its time covering such life-cycle dramas, film narratives that focus on the protagonist's rite(s) of passage cluster instead around certain dramatic hinge moments (leaving home, meeting new people, facing particular emotional challenges, etc.). The older, wiser main character of the *Bildungsfilm* will look back at their youth in an attempt to present it as a coherently as possibly to the audience while at the same time seeking to understand it themselves in the context of their current situation. Frequently, the protagonist of the *Bildungsfilm* will narrate the unfolding story via a voiceover.[2]

In *The Spanish Apartment*, that voiceover is an important device. As the narrator of his own life story, Xavier leads the audience from episode to episode, sometimes commenting at length on particular incidents (his arrival in Barcelona, the interview, etc.) to provide an introspective feel to this auto-biography. Midway through *The Spanish Apartment*, Xavier recalls that in Barcelona, each harrowing ordeal will become an adventure, and for some idiotic reason, your most horrific experiences are the stories you most love to tell. Klapisch does not dwell on the harrowing and the horrific in *The Spanish Apartment* – he portrays Xavier's romantic and emotional entanglements as awkward dilemmas rather than debilitating traumas. However, these are still events happening to Xavier for the first time, in an unfamiliar environment, away from the security of home and family. Viewed through his eyes, his ordeals *at the time* clearly have an effect on him, and it is only through the writing of 'The Spanish Apartment' a year after he left Paris that these encounters can be processed with a degree of retrospective maturity. In her analysis of nostalgic coming-of-age films, Lesley Speed (1998) notes that the nostalgic teen film tends to be structured around a young male's acquisition of maturity and/or masculinity. This tension is caused by the fact that while most teen films emphasize an adolescent point of view, the nostalgia film privileges an adult's memory of past events; and in its emphasis on past events, the nostalgic teen film expresses 'a desire for moral and ideological security' (1998: 24).

The first eight minutes of the film detail, in rapid fashion, the circumstances behind Xavier's move from Paris to Barcelona. He lives at home with his ex-hippy mother (who berates him for only ever eating fast food). He has a girlfriend, Martine (Audrey Tautou), who is named after the heroine of a children's book, *Martine à la ferme/Martine on the Farm*.[3] He tells us that as a boy, he used to be blonde and wanted to be a writer. Now he looks like Romain Duris and is drifting half-heartedly towards an EU civil service job. To the sounds of Grégoire Charpentier's 'Te Deum' (c. 1688), he visits Jean-Charles Perrin (Wladimir Yordanoff), an old friend of his father's at the Ministry of Finance in Paris. Over cigars and expensive malt whisky,[4] Perrin tells Xavier that once he finishes his *Diplôme d'études approfondies* (*DEA*, the French equivalent of Honors), he can come and work for him. Xavier will also need to speak Spanish because Spain is where most of the new job opportunities are to be found.

Xavier enrolls in the Erasmus program and completes his application in Paris. 'What an unspeakable mess (*bordel*)' is how Xavier first describes the program. While Klapisch has always been a strong advocate for youth mobility across Europe, he undercuts the fluid, frictionless aspects of the scheme with an early comic scene which involves Xavier dealing with unco-operative secretaries who have neither the time nor the inclination to explain the application process to him. Instead, he is required to fill out reams of paperwork and is shuttled from one administrative building to another. To visualize this bureaucratic muddle, Klapisch deploys a series of tessellated split screens and accelerated tracking shots as we follow Xavier down corridors and into offices and crams the screen with multicolored files and forms and papers and *pièces d'identité*, layering more and more of them over the screen until Xavier is literally engulfed by the paperwork required for his stay in Spain. This is Jerry Pournelle's 'Iron Law of Bureaucracy' (2006) writ large: red tape is crushingly mundane, generating doubt and confusion.[5] Xavier's voiceover (interspersed with overhead shots of busy motorway interchanges) reinforces the point:

> I don't know how the world became such a mess [. . .] Why did it have to be this way? Complicated, made like shit, out of whack. Before there were fields, cows, chickens. It was much simpler. They had a direct relationship with things.

Cue a familiar lament. Klapisch's previous films also offered a critique of relentless progress, urban renewal and bureaucratic 'streamlining' (*Little Nothings*, *When the Cat's Away*), and in *The Spanish Apartment*, he suggests that the emerging young French generation is being held to ransom by the maze-like complexity of modern life and the intractable notion that all change is positive. In a negative review of Klapisch's 2008 film *Paris*, Peter Bradshaw remarked how the film conformed to French commercial cinema's tendency to veer into the over-sweetened and picturesque, a kind of nostalgia for an idealized present (Bradshaw 2008). Bradshaw is mobilizing a discourse around the deployment of nostalgia in contemporary French cinema that has become increasingly widespread in the last decade. Sébastien Fevry prefers the term 'sepia cinema': those restorative, cohesive films which project the image of an ideal past in a French society more and more obsessed with its own memory and the valorization of its national past (2017: 60–61).[6] Though neither *Paris* nor *The Spanish Apartment* is directly affiliated to Fevry's formulation, Klapisch's films frequently trade in these push-pull forces between past, present and future. In *When the Cat's Away*, a wide variety of neighbors from a tightly delineated area of Paris rally into action when a young woman's cat disappears. This notion of the city as a collection of mutually supportive micro-communities trying to shield itself from the inexorable forces of consumerism and fast-disappearing *quartiers* obliquely resurfaces in *The Spanish Apartment*.

Klapisch has, very economically, programmed by now the basic narrative coordinates of his *Bildungsroman*. Our hero is melancholic ('I'm sad, everyone's sad', he tells his mother) and evidently in search of some kind of purpose to his life beyond the probable professional trajectory mapped out for people of his age. He is in a perfunctory relationship with Martine and has difficulty communicating with his mother and father. His world is out of whack, static like the cars frozen in time in the large, framed picture behind Perrin's office desk. He has been to Ibiza once and speaks *un poquito español*. Several oppositions have been constructed, some of which will form further narrative tensions later on the film: France vs. Spain; ex-hippy mother vs. *énarque* father;[7] being a writer or working in an office; restriction vs. freedom, and so on. The Paris that Xavier is leaving behind is not the Paris of *Amélie* or *When the Cat's Away*. The city here is a place of drudgery, monotony and conformity. Life is lived amidst what Marc Augé has termed 'non-places': spaces within our 'supermodern' world which are 'formed in relation to certain ends (transport, transit, commerce, leisure)' (1995: 94). Klapisch densely layers this opening section of the film with images of corridors, lobbies, lifts, road interchanges and airport lounges, and Xavier is frequently seen passing through these spaces in an accelerated, choppy fashion. For Augé, an individual who enters a non-place

> is relieved of his usual determinants. He becomes no more than what he does or experiences in the role of passenger, customer, or driver. [. . .] *The space of non-place creates neither singular identity nor relations; only solitude, and similitude.* There is no room for history unless it has been transformed into an element of spectacle, usually in allusive texts.
>
> (1995: 103, my emphasis)

Xavier leaves Paris lacking an identity or at the very least possessing a conflicting one. He is caught between two worlds, each epitomized by his parents, between on the one hand self-expression and freedom and on the other conformity and the fulfilment of parental expectations. This tension is reflected in Xavier's clothing. Here, he is buttoned up both literally and figuratively. There is the conservative haircut, muted color of his jumper and the shirt tucked into his trousers. At the airport, he cries as he leaves his mother and Martine behind and cries again on the plane. We sense that Xavier is leaving one life behind and creating a new one. His journey is beginning, his identity already starting to fragment.[8]

'Xavier Rousseau's apprenticeship'

Enda McCaffrey and Murray Pratt (2011: 439) note how throughout the film 'the ghost of France haunts [Xavier's] every step'. And so it proves at the baggage carousel at Barcelona airport. Xavier's first conversation is with a French couple, Jean-Michel (Xavier de Guillebon) and his new wife Anne-Sophie (Judith Godrèche). Jean-Michel prepares Xavier for the fun in store for him as a young Erasmus student: 'You're going to have a blast [. . .] Not even the cats eat before 10pm. Barcelona's people are real party animals [. . .] Erasmus is pretty intense [. . .] You won't sleep much!' Ezra and Sánchez (2005) read this limited focus on the hedonism of Barcelona as a reductive device used throughout *The Spanish Apartment* to sidestep any closer engagement with current social and cultural shifts in Spain – here, 'partying, sex, drugs and aesthetic design seem to be all' (146). Jean-Michel is already hinting at the lifestyle that awaits in the city and the various emotional predicaments he will be involved in (and, given that Xavier will shortly cuckold the other man, it is a highly ironic comment). More immediately pressing for Xavier is his impatience to leave Jean-Michel's company, representing as he does the kind of hyper-privileged bourgeois Frenchman he is looking to flee from. Xavier disembarks the airport shuttle bus, and takes his first steps in Barcelona. He observes, via voiceover:

> When you first arrive in a new city, nothing makes sense. Everything's unknown, virgin [. . .] After you've lived here, walked these streets, you'll know them inside out. You'll know these people. Once you've lived here, walked these streets this street 10, 20, 1000 times [. . .] it'll belong to you because you've lived there. That was about to happen to me, but I didn't know it yet.

Slowly but surely, Xavier is becoming the classic *flâneur* (stroller, wanderer), the figure first mentioned in Charles Baudelaire's 1863 essay 'The Painter of Modern Life'. Described as a passionate spectator, the (male) *flâneur* wandered the streets of nineteenth-century Paris looking at, listening to and taking in all aspects of modern metropolitan life; one who moves through the streets and hidden spaces of the city, placing himself in the middle of the action but remaining somehow detached and apart from it (1964: 9). The typical *flâneur*, referred to by Baudelaire as Monsieur C.G., is a man of the world in that he understands the mysterious and lawful reasons for all its uses (7). This knowledge, Baudelaire argues, is the result of Monsieur C.G.'s approach to life, or an intense, childlike curiosity that allows him to see everything in a state of newness (8).

Though an outsider, Xavier's first few moments in Barcelona seem to confirm his *flâneur* status: he takes the bus from the airport, not a taxi; he asks for directions in Spanish; he walks the streets with his map and with his luggage (note that as well as pulling a suitcase behind him, Xavier also awkwardly wears one rucksack on his back and one on his front in classic 'student traveler' mode). He crosses the Plaça Reial, and Klapisch frames him inside a red circle with an arrow and the legend '*Je suis ici*/Here I am'. Though still an outsider, he is gradually asserting his presence on the topography of Barcelona. Shot in close-up, mid-shot or long shot (to both focus on his immediate sense impressions and embed him in the urban environment), Xavier, to paraphrase Walter Benjamin, calmly and adventurously goes traveling. Earlier, when Perrin had asked Xavier if he knew Spain, Xavier had replied that he had been to Ibiza and '*habla un poquito español*' ('speaks a little Spanish'). Yet as soon as he arrives, he seeks to 'fit in'. Unlike William, who arrives later in the film and wreaks havoc, Xavier is a good traveler rather than a crass tourist or 'free-floating individual' (Elliot and Urry 2010: 54) who looks only for superficial encounters with the local culture. He is not 'lost'; rather he is adrift, seeking to navigate the streets, take on the language, and master the cultural norms of the city. A group of street kids may taunt him – '*vete a tu país*' ('go back to your own country'), they shout to him as he struggles with his luggage – but Xavier remains undaunted. In his famous piece on the redemption of physical reality, Siegfried Kracauer developed Baudelaire's ideas, asserting that:

> the street in the extended sense of the word is not only the arena of fleeting impressions and chance encounters but a place where the flow of life is bound to assert itself [. . .] What appeals to him [the *flâneur*] are not so much sharp-contoured individuals engaged in this or that definable pursuit as loose throngs of sketchy, completely indeterminate figures [. . .] The *flâneur* is intoxicated with life in the street.
>
> (1960: 72)

In this opening period, Xavier's relationship to the city is not yet fixed but, like his sense of identity and belonging, ever-evolving. His sensitivity to the sights and sounds of Barcelona are already becoming heightened, even if he is not yet fully aware of his growing interdependence with the city.

With the youthful glee of a *flâneur*, Xavier absorbs the foreign sounds of the metro stations and street names: 'Urquinaona, which sounded Sioux, was added to the list of once bizarre-sounding names tucked into my brain [. . .] Honolulu, Punxsutawney, Piccadilly, Massachusetts, Saskatoon and Machu Picchu. It became normal and familiar'. In a turn reminiscent of Michel de Certeau's notion that street and place names lose their official signification as inhabitants generate their own meanings, Xavier demonstrates here how city wanderers who take pleasure in walking the streets can subsequently invent their own spaces through their interactions with them: 'they detach themselves from the places they were supposed to define and serve as imaginary meeting points on itineraries which, as metaphors, they determine for reasons that are foreign to their original value but may be recognized or not by passers-by' (1988: 104). Xavier's process of acculturation is underway. And then, to cap this opening section in Barcelona, as if by magic, as he waits to cross a busy road, a future version of Xavier walks directly towards us/him. This new Xavier has changed: he walks slowly, confidently, with a new hairstyle, T-shirt and tanned skin, at ease with himself and in his surroundings. Like the flash-forwarding images of Xavier's interactions with his future friends embedded in Brocherie's credit sequence, Klapisch symbolically blends two distinct moments – right now and an undefined future – to hint that Xavier's stay in Barcelona will be more than just passing time. This Xavier 2.0 walking towards us is an idealized future version of the current Xavier – not just tourist, not just student, not just French, not just 'emerging adult', but all of these overlapping identities.

Xavier's cultural adjustments to his new life in the city continue. At one point, Xavier goes to dinner with Anne-Sophie and Jean-Michel, and they tell him how they met: at a pizzeria in Dinard on the northwest coast of France. Jean-Michel tells Xavier that the Italian owner spoke with an exaggerated French accent. On hearing this, Xavier looks visibly uncomfortable. His intercultural sensitivity is fast emerging, and the fact that a fellow Frenchman has uttered this barely concealed snobbery seems to offend him even more. At the Iposa bar, Xavier is told to visit there more often by Juan, the owner. This is where you'll learn about the real Barcelona and learn to talk *puta madre* Spanish from the locals, he tells Xavier. Klapisch suggests that there are creative tensions at play here between the different 'Barcelonas' that Xavier interacts with. There is the tourist city, the Erasmus city, the real city, and so on. Learning swear words – that is, becoming a real local – can ultimately only be achieved by turning away from the iconic landmarks of the city, refuting the compromised, often rigid directives of study abroad and Erasmus travel and diving headfirst into the messy reality of Barcelona. For Mariana Liz, Xavier's relationship with the city remains dual: he is 'in' (knows the names of some places, recognizes routes and buildings), yet he is also 'out'. In spatial terms, the film oscillates between a defense of authenticity (wanting to know the 'real' Barcelona) and the perpetuation of stereotypes (including in his 'to-see-before leaving' list places such as Montjuïc) (Liz 2016: 120).

Xavier's growing 'insider' status in the film is thrown into sharp relief by his ongoing interactions with Martine and Anne-Sophie. While in Barcelona, Xavier becomes less reserved and more eloquent towards his girlfriend and is now able to express his feelings in letters to Martine far more openly and honestly than before. It seems at first that the distance – both geographic and emotional – between them will revitalize their relationship. Yet as soon as Martine visits Xavier in Barcelona, and spends time with his flatmates, it is clear that things are not right. She describes Wendy as 'goofy' and 'super uptight'; she doesn't like his room ('you made it sound so blissful, but this . . .') and is unable to have sex with Xavier because she doesn't feel at home. Klapisch then cuts to their departure at the airport as she returns to Paris. This time, it's not tearful, as it was when Xavier left her in Paris a few months earlier. They part as strangers. Later, while Xavier is visiting his favorite bar in Barcelona, she rings him, angrily upbraiding him for not coming to Paris for her birthday. By this point, there seems nothing left to salvage in their relationship, and Klapisch reinforces the point by cutting between a sunny Barcelona and a grey, rain-swept Paris. As McCaffrey and Pratt (2011: 439) remind us, Martine's presence at the end of the phone is one of several visual, vocal and imaginary memories of humdrum France that periodically snap Xavier out of his Spanish life and pull him back home, his new identity still unfinished.

Xavier's gradual shift towards maturation is further offset by the attitudes of Anne-Sophie. Though she and Xavier are similar in age (Godrèche was twenty-nine when filming began), she displays none of his youthful curiosity or cultural inquisitiveness. If he plunges into life in Barcelona, she is the embodiment of the anti-*flâneur*, scared to leave her apartment, unwilling to learn the language: 'It scares me [. . .] Like I'm about to climb a huge mountain'. She is a typical Parisian BCBG:[9] well dressed, elegant, aloof, slightly dull. At one point, Xavier takes Anne-Sophie to the Iposa (he is a regular there now), and she is clearly uneasy. When the two of them walk through Barcelona, she describes it as being such a dirty city.[10] Xavier reproaches her for what he perceives to be her insularity and cultural snobbery (both key themes for Klapisch). She asks Xavier if he think she's old-fashioned and repressed (*coincée*); 'you're at ease everywhere, all the time', she tells him. She is confirming not just her outside status, an unadventurous visitor ill-equipped to step outside of her comfort zone, but also underlining Xavier's growing ability to feel part of the city. One of the key drivers of *The Spanish Apartment* is collective malleability, namely, how different nationalities, cultural identities and languages can coexist and cope with changes both negative and positive within a specific environment. As we can see, Xavier is becoming increasingly adaptable – emotionally resilient, culturally keen and by now an integral part of the local community. Conversely, Anne-Sophie is far more reserved and closed off from the community. Godrèche's body language conveys this hesitation: she sits with legs and arms crossed, she uses the polite '*vous*' form even when speaking to Xavier, has no desire to leave the apartment, and faints at the top of the Sagrada Família.

As Jeffrey Arnett reminds us, 'emerging adults often explore a variety of possible life directions in love, work and worldviews' (2004: 469); in Xavier's case, his 'emerging adult' period in Barcelona is a sexual rite of passage as much as an emotional and cultural one. Despite her uptight nature, Anne-Sophie plays a crucial role in Xavier's sexual initiation. Xavier leaves Martine behind in Paris and over the course of his year in Barcelona becomes increasingly sexually confident. It starts with the affair with Anne-Sophie, but he also struggles to conceal his romantic feelings towards Isabelle – which are only thwarted when he tells her that she is a lesbian. He ends his year in Barcelona tentatively beginning a relationship with Neus (Irene Montalà), a Spanish waitress at the Iposa.[11] Earlier, Martine had told Xavier that his fantasy is 'a nice little girl in a short skirt [and] rosy cheeks', in other words, a compliant, attractive version of a woman epitomized by Anne-Sophie. At one point, images of Anne-Sophie wearing lingerie and calling out his name flash into Xavier's mind while he is working on an assignment about stock options. It seems that sexual opportunity is everywhere in Barcelona. It's hinted at by Jean-Michel at the airport. William interrupts Xavier in the apartment one day to explain the mating rituals of a fly. Isabelle has a fling with her female flamenco teacher (whose sexual confidence is exemplified by the eroticized flamenco music she dances to). Despite Isabelle's lesbianism, the rapport between her and Xavier seems so amorous that she confesses that she wishes he were a girl. 'The world is badly made' is Xavier's reply. He is angry towards Wendy when she begins her casual fling with Bruce, which suggests that he also has feelings towards her (while these feelings remain unspoken in *The Spanish Apartment*, eventually Wendy and Xavier will become lovers in *Russian Dolls* and divorced parents in *Chinese Puzzle*). Isabelle teaches him how to seduce women in a way that is both forceful and intimate; later on, Xavier will then use those skills to seduce Anne-Sophie to the sounds of a Chopin waltz. Yet despite this newly acquired sexual experience, Xavier still behaves like an unreconstructed adolescent when he recounts to Isabelle how easy it was to seduce Anne-Sophie with her advice and how, when he next sees her, he will be more sexually aggressive. Isabelle's response cuts him down very quickly: 'Don't talk like that'. Despite his conquest, Xavier is still puerile.

Figure 3.2 'The world is badly made' – unrequited love between Xavier and Isabelle
Image courtesy of Photofest

Life in the apartment

Klapisch's focus on youthful behavior and attitudes narrows as soon as Xavier moves into the 'Spanish apartment'. For many nostalgic spectators, this all-too-familiar depiction of student life in the apartment remains the most memorable aspect of the film: the (failed) romances, the studying, the cultural misunderstandings and the subtle, comic stereotypes. It's not until the twenty-second minute of *The Spanish Apartment* that we first enter the apartment. Xavier is about to undergo an interview with the other five flatmates. 'This isn't a trial', says Wendy to Xavier, but of course it is).[12] Xavier badly wants to be accepted into group. He has already been to several apartment openings in Barcelona, only to be faced with exorbitant rent prices, down-at-heel rooms and long lines of potential renters ahead of him in the queue. His body language is expectant. Klapisch films Duris front on, and through a series of shot/reverse shots the camera adopts Xavier's viewpoint, tracking and spinning from one person to the next as they question him or talk to each other. He is overwhelmed by the energy and exuberance of his prospective flatmates, smiling nervously and agreeing with everything that is said. Straightaway, the group dynamics in the apartment are coded as chaotic, full of contradiction, but never dysfunctional. Tobias tells Xavier that 'we want life to be cool together, we want good vibes between people', but then Alessandro complains that it might be difficult to have a French person in the apartment because not everyone speaks French. Lars then counters this by arguing that the group never said that nationality would be a problem. Within a few moments, an innocuous interview has degenerated into petty squabbling and entrenched national positions. 'I loved this place. I'd have given anything to be accepted', Xavier concludes in voiceover. In the Maslowian sense, Xavier is moving up through his 'hierarchy of needs' towards social belonging, esteem and self-actualization.

The acceptance by the others and his move into the apartment confirms the next stage in Xavier's progressing development and is the cue for Radiohead's mournful song 'No Surprises' (1997) to play on the soundtrack. The song is played three times in *The Spanish Apartment*. Scott Henderson has argued that music in teen films is 'foregrounded as a primary marker of character' and that instead of supplementing or commenting upon the narrative, the director's musical choices are often a 'main concern of the central characters' (2006: 149). The lyrics for 'No Surprises' reveal a duality at the heart of Xavier's maturation: 'A heart that's full up like a landfill/A job that slowly kills you/Bruises that won't heal/You look so tired and unhappy [. . .] I'll take a quiet life/A handshake of carbon monoxide'. As the soundtrack for such a momentous step in Xavier's new life in Barcelona, it seems an odd choice of song. It continues to play as Xavier puts two photographs on the wall of his new room: one is the black-and-white photo of him as a small boy that we saw earlier in his mother's flat (complete with Xavier's voiceover: 'I want to write books'); the other is of him and Martine. We hear it again as Klapisch flash-forwards to the scene of Xavier sitting at his desk preparing to write. It is a visual echo of the same image we saw during the credit sequence, only this time the image is intercut with other scenes of his new flatmates going about their daily routines in the apartment – coming home with the shopping, reading, studying, relaxing in their rooms. There is a final cut back to the computer screen, revealing the title of Xavier's book – '*L'auberge espagnole*' – before the song fades out. Fiona Handyside has observed that recent French films by female directors incorporate particular types of music 'to enhance the emotional and affective intensity of audience engagement with the girls' subjectivity' (2016: 124). Klapisch achieves a similar sonic aim here with the inclusion of Radiohead.[13] The move into the flat is the catalyst for Xavier's acceptance by the group, but the music adds a trace of sadness as he prepares to leave one life behind to begin another.

Apart from Xavier, we learn very little about the characters in *The Spanish Apartment*. However, given Klapisch's fondness for groups and microcommunities, each flatmate is given a series of short scenes in which his or her personality is sketched out. Foibles and national tics are first used to delineate the characters and then to show that any difference that does exist can be easily bridged. Nothing seems insurmountable here. Rents are raised, there is a power cut, relationships break down, the bathroom plughole is full of hair, but everything, for Klapisch, can be reconciled. A. O. Scott (2003) in the *New York Times* noticed how the film offered 'an appealing and persuasive picture of European integration, in which national differences, which once sparked military and political conflict, are preserved because they make life sexier and more interesting'. Indeed, for such a messy melting pot, the only 'conflicts' we see inside the apartment are minor domestic skirmishes. Crisps are dropped on the floor, the bathroom is not cleaned properly, the dishes are not done, and Alessandro and Lars smoke joints in Wendy's room because it's the only clean place in the apartment. All of these scenes suggest how differences can be unified. Cohabitation is the catalyst for mutual cooperation and understanding, suggests Klapisch. Europe's young, emerging adult generation may speak different languages and hold fast to different cultures, but the clashes that exist between them can be brooked.

In fact, it is an external tension that most notably intrudes on this domestic *pax Europeana* and one that epitomizes 'Old Europe'. The landlord arrives unannounced to raise the rent; he is deeply unimpressed by the pizza boxes and empty beer cans and the fact that his icon of the Virgin Mary has been replaced by a green robot and there are pictures of Erasmus with graffiti on the wall. The flatmates hide behind a bedroom door, their heads peeking out one of top of the other through a crack in the door as the landlord patrols the apartment (this shot became the film's international marketing image). Xavier is thrust into the role of diplomat and peacemaker, telling the older man that 'we're young [. . .] but we're responsible'. The landlord's reply – 'from now on, I'm dealing with you' – demonstrates another sign of Xavier's growing transition to adulthood.

In his famous book *Imagined Communities* (1983), Benedict Anderson suggested that a nation is a socially constructed community, 'imagined' by the people who see themselves as part of that community. Anderson defines the nation as 'an imagined political community – and imagined as both inherently limited and sovereign [. . .] It is imagined because the members of even the smallest nation will never know most of their fellow-members, meet them, or even hear of them, yet in the minds of each lives the image of their communion' (1983: 6). In this sense, *The Spanish Apartment* is about adaptability, about 'fitting in' and feeling part of a wider 'imagined community'. The apartment, and by extension cosmopolitan cities like Barcelona, is not bound by the intractability of national languages or borders. The flatmates, regardless of nationality, 'belong' in and to this space, connected to their fellow 'strangers' (*étrangers*) through shared values and emotions. Klapisch is clearly impressed by the way the European project can accommodate, assimilate and integrate national cultures within the 'apartment' while at the same time allowing individual tics, traits and national characteristics to come to the fore. The subdivided refrigerator, with clearly demarcated sections for each flatmate, quickly becomes a chaotic jumble, with items haphazardly

Figure 3.3 Hiding from the landlord
Image courtesy of Alamy

stacked in the wrong place. Xavier's voiceover comment – 'the refrigerator sorted itself out' – is revealing here for it suggests once more that the messy dynamics of communal coexistence are both inevitable and preferable to the symbolic segregation created by borders, zones and refrigerator racks.

Mobility and linguistic interaction for the seven apartment dwellers is remarkably easy – borders from one country to another are crossed effortlessly; the lingua franca flips between Spanish and English, languages with which all are comfortable; and there are no concerted efforts by the students to learn any other languages. Indeed, languages other than Spanish and English represented in the apartment are reduced to a multilingual notice affixed to the wall next to the communal phone. It reads – in Italian, Danish, French and German – as well as English and Spanish: '[Name] is not here. [She/He] will be back this evening'. Linguistic confusion rarely happens in this somewhat limited multilingual environment, and when it does, Klapisch exploits it for obvious comic purposes. Wendy answers the telephone and has a conversation with Xavier's mother:

Wendy: Xavier's gone to school. Okay?
Xavier's mother: Ah, oui! Il est à la fac.
W: What?
XM: La fac!
W: La fuck?!
XM: Yes. After fac he can telephone maman.

The humor here stems from Wendy's misunderstanding of the French word for university – *la faculté*, or *la fac*.

Language, identity, stereotype

Klapisch has always been unambiguous about his deliberate deployment of mild stereotypes and clichés in *The Spanish Apartment*, and throughout he sprinkles scenes that raise wider debates about identity politics and the politics of the melting pot. For example, at their first Erasmus class, Xavier and Isabelle attend a lecture on the future of global capitalism that the lecturer proceeds to deliver in Catalan. Isabelle asks the lecturer to speak in Castilian (i.e. Spanish), but he replies that because most of the students present are Catalan, he should not have to switch languages. Their exchange is revealing:

Isabelle: We are more than fifteen Erasmus students who don't speak Catalan, and it's easy for you to speak Spanish.
Lecturer: I understand your position perfectly, miss. Really, perfectly. But you have to understand mine as well. We're in Catalonia and here Catalan is the official language. If you want to speak Spanish, go to Madrid or South America.

Klapisch here draws attention to the role of regional and linguistic identity, which may become more prominent in a unified Europe than within a discrete nation-state. That's why, at a café after the lecture, Isabelle complains to other local and Erasmus students that it is contradictory to defend Catalan at the very moment they're creating a European Union. She is adopting the traditional line of argument that asserts that a nation's dominant language should also be its principal language. Yet European identity can exist alongside a national identity. Indeed, historically, the ideas for a 'united Europe' put forward in the nineteenth century by the likes of Guiseppe Mazzini and

Victor Hugo were not designed to create a homogenous nation-state but rather to plant a unified Europe *alongside* the individual nation. Contrary to Isabelle's complaint, the idea of Europe is always to go beyond nationalism. To confirm this, a Catalan student of Gambian origin responds to Isabelle:

> I don't agree. First of all, because we're discussing identity. There's not one single valid identity, but many varied and perfectly compatible identities. It's a question of respect [. . .] I have at least two identities: my Gambian identity, which I carry internally, and my Catalan identity. It's not contradictory to combine identities.

Amago notes that Barcelona's local traditions, language and culture 'are unique, but these local characteristics are part of a larger, globalized identity that transcends the purely national' (2007: 22). Here, the Gambian student is reiterating Barcelona's hybridized, globalized identity, corroborating Klapisch's decision to the set *The Spanish Apartment* in the city because of its multiple, overlapping identities and cultures. Isabelle's viewpoint suggests that for her, the 'new Europe' is a process of eliding national differences and linguistic/identity formulations (this is itself an inconsistent position, given that Isabelle is a French-speaking Belgian).[14] Then, two Spanish and Catalan students talk about how individuals may embrace multiple identities and express those apparent contradictions both bilingually and multiculturally. They gesture to Xavier: 'You're French. You're not Martian [. . .] you cherish your French identity. You identify with Astérix, Françoise Hardy and cheese'; while another notes: 'Spain isn't just *olé*. It's not just flamenco. It's lots of things and Catalan is one of them'. Identity can never just be predicated on cultural clichés and bland stereotypes despite the best efforts of Wendy's brother. Klapisch has commented that

> I played with the clichés. For instance, since we were in Spain, I put in a Flamenco scene. But since I found it was a bit ridiculous, I add a sentence of the guy who says 'Spain is not only flamenco'. [. . .] Besides, everything is a bit exaggerated. The characters are very stereotyped, and so are the situations.
>
> (quoted in Béguin 2004: 74)

For Klapisch, 'one of the themes in this film is to convey the identity of each country', and therefore it was 'necessary to handle the clichés to show what's inside' (74) using humor and irony. For example, most of the apartment treats Bruce, the American guitar player with whom Wendy has a relationship, condescendingly. Xavier even refers to him as 'that stupid American', even though we never learn enough about Bruce to justify Xavier's disdain.

However, the internal stability of the apartment is eventually thrown into disarray by the arrival of Wendy's brother, William, who comes to visit. As soon as he arrives, the convivial and generally harmonious atmosphere among the flatmates quickly sours, and 'the good vibes' that were so very important to Tobias turn hostile. William antagonizes the flatmates at dinner, coarsely recounting a conversation he had with the Spanish train conductor and spouting random words in Spanish. Needless to say, Soledad is not impressed:

William: He said, *Corrida. Vamos a la playa.* Or something like that, and I didn't understand it. So I said to him, just trying to be funny, have a chat, I said, *Olé, muchacho! Caramba!*, you know.

Soledad: We don't say *Caramba* here in Spain.

W.: Oh. Spanish people, they seem to be very proud, don't they?

S.: Did you meet a lot of Spanish people so far?

W.: No I didn't. Just that guy on the train. And you.

S.: So how can you generalize about Spanish people?

W.: Well, no, no, I'm not. But, you know what I'm saying, don't you?

S.: Sure. *Me gustan mucho tu monologos* [I love your monologues]. *Olé.*

As Jane Warren notes, we dismiss William as a one-dimensional, largely unsympathetic character based on these first few moments. He is not arrogant, or xenophobic or destructive but rather ignorant, as confirmed by Soledad's sarcastic final line. William trades in variations of the same stereotypes the Spanish and Catalan students had earlier used as examples to ironically critique the reductive capacity of the national cliché. His *faux pas* means he remains an 'outsider', on the periphery of the group in the apartment and, in Klapisch's eyes, of Europe as a whole (Warren 2008). William's recourse to national stereotypes does not stop here. Later, he enters Tobias's room and notes that his side of the room is much tidier than Alessandro's: 'You Germans, you like order, don't you?'. Cue an Adolf Hitler gag and the eye-rollingly embarrassing scene of William goose-stepping round the room. It's shortly after this scene that everyone in the apartment bar Wendy wants William to leave.

The gentle ribbing between flatmates has been replaced by a far more overt, casual racism. As Béguin notes, William 'does not perceive the foreigners as individuals, but as foreigners of a certain type. This foreign origin, which prevails over the other dimensions of an identity, works as a symbolic border'

(2004: 74). William is inexperienced. He is the odd one out. He leaves the nightclub with the other students and drunkenly proceeds to vomit and urinate in the street. To paraphrase Stephen George's (1990) description of the difficult relationship between Britain and its European allies, he is the 'awkward partner' in the apartment. But let us not forget that William is also the youngest character in the film. He is not yet an 'emerging adult' but still trapped in that liminal state between child and adolescent. He has not yet been exposed to cultural and linguistic opportunities that Wendy is able to take advantage of so readily. William's own rite of passage will not be kick-started while on his travels to Barcelona but later on, back in London, while working at the Royal Albert Hall. We shall eventually, and somewhat surprisingly, witness the outcome of William's maturation in *Russian Dolls*.

Existential slumps

On his return to the apartment after breaking up with Martine in Paris, Xavier is slumped on the sofa, watching a television program about human towers. The tower, or *castell*, is an important part of Catalan culture, often performed in public spaces in front of thousands of spectators. *Castellers* arrange themselves into multiple levels, starting at the base with a mass of people, gradually rising up to ten levels, and topping out the tower with a small child. In 2010, such *castells* were recognized by UNESCO as an integral part of Catalan cultural identity, 'transmitted from generation to generation and providing community members a sense of continuity, social cohesion and solidarity' (Massallé 2014). Watching on the sofa with Xavier are three other flatmates – Lars, Alessandro and Isabelle – each of whom is deep in an existential funk.

So why might Klapisch include an image of the *castell* here, if only briefly? Partly, I suggest, to culturally locate the film and provide some local color. Partly too to offer a visual shorthand for the students' ennui, zoned out on the sofa, surrounded by empty pizza boxes and beer cans, sharing cigarettes. Each of them has just ended a relationship – Xavier with Martine, Lars with his partner, who has unexpectedly turned up in Barcelona with his baby, and Isabelle with her Belgian lover. The *castell* is also a useful metaphor for the developing friendships and shared emotional experiences of this moment among the quartet. The *castellers'* motto is *força, equilibri, valor i seny* (strength, balance, courage and common sense): the *castell* will rise or fall depending on robust foundations, good internal balance, the structural support of others and the trust required to safely build the castell higher and higher. Likewise, for the 'Spanish apartment' to flourish requires mutual understanding and empathy. If the flatmates do not always display common sense, then that is perhaps the ultimate point that Klapisch is making here in his coming-of-age tale – the getting of common sense, good judgment, and wisdom is the ultimate goal of the hero of the *Bildungsroman*. Building the perfect *castell* takes planning and thought. It takes time.

Xavier's depression refuses to right itself, and he decides to have an MRI scan at Jean-Michel's hospital to reassure himself. During the scan, Klapisch includes a dream sequence that culminates with Xavier being unable to speak French anymore. He has lost all ties with his mother tongue and therefore France and his French identity (we have been primed for this existential crisis – earlier, standing in the sea at the coastal town of Sitges with Jean-Michel and Anne-Sophie, Xavier asks, 'Which way is France?'). The loss of French recalls an earlier conversation with Jean-Michel, who had explained how people can lose the ability to speak a second language after a bang to the head or a fall. Xavier's fall here is now visualized by a hallucinatory brain-washing process in which men with sledgehammers break down the walls in his brain under the guidance of Jean-Michel ('let's clean up that mess'). The camera pans and swirls over papers, sticky notes and books, and the sequence ends with Xavier's face turning redder and redder as Jean-Michel finally realizes that he has been having an affair with Anne-Sophie. Showcasing Klapisch's visual élan and fondness for unconventional, surrealistic narrative swerves, the scene also visualizes in abstract terms both Xavier's identity loss and identity building during his rite of passage. There have been rapid, sustained spikes in his linguistic, cultural and emotional development in Barcelona, and here we see the extent to which Xavier is marooned between two cultures – no longer 'French' but not yet quite 'Spanish'.

Figure 3.4 Building a *castell*

Leaving

Eventually, the members of the apartment all work together to save Wendy. Her boyfriend Alistair has arrived unannounced in Barcelona and is on his way to meet Wendy. She is in bed with Bruce and does not hear the flat's telephone ringing to tell her that Alistair is on his way. It's now a race against time as the flatmates must band together to warn Wendy and distract Alistair without arousing his suspicion. It is the major set piece of the film and demonstrates the solidarity and group friendship that now exists among the flatmates. Klapisch uses split screens and wipes to indicate the developing stages of the incident and the mounting suspense (Alistair on the bus, Wendy in bed with Bruce, Xavier running back to the flat, Tobias pretending the keys don't work).[15] It is William who saves the day, jumping into bed with Bruce just as Alistair opens the door to Wendy's room. It is a moment of Feydeauesque farce in which sexual infidelity is covered up and an existing relationship (tentatively?) recuperated. Klapisch also gently 'punishes' William – the boorish, rampantly heterosexual 'Englishman abroad' is rebuked for his earlier insensitive behavior and forced to pretend to be gay and wear a pink silk dressing gown to salvage his sister's honor and finally gain the respect of the flatmates. That festival atmosphere continues into the final departure scene at the Iposa bar. All of Xavier's friends are in attendance as the group prepares to head back home. Benedict Anderson's conception of the nation materializes once more – the apartment as his version of the 'imagined community' reveals itself in this final scene 'as a deep, horizontal comradeship' (Anderson 1983: 3).

In the sequel, *Russian Dolls*, this community remain friends and will reunite for a wedding. For Klapisch, they represent a flourishing generation of pan-European citizens, and by bringing together the main characters in the 2005 sequel, he recaps one of his central themes – adaptability. By now, all in the apartment have learned a literal and figurative new language, are comfortable spending time in local bars and enter into a direct engagement with the city, its people and its customs. Xavier is given the red T-shirt we saw in the credit sequence as a leaving gift. Anne-Sophie and Jean-Michel say good-bye,[16] there is a rapprochement between William and Tobias, Xavier embraces the Gambian-Catalan student and Wendy cries. She, like the rest of the apartment, senses that something has ended. She does not know it yet, but for some in the apartment, that comradeship will last longer than any of them can imagine.

Xavier returns to Paris and his *Bildungsroman* trajectory is complete. He is a changed man. When his mother asks him about Barcelona, he replies, deflated, that 'it was great'. Xavier is suffering from an acute sense of 'reverse culture shock', in other words, the process of readjusting, re-acculturating, and re-assimilating into one's own home culture after living in a different culture for a significant period of time (Gaw 2000: 83–84). The psychological, emotional and cultural aspects of reentry from one environment to another can be highly stressful, with common side effects including academic problems, cultural identity conflict, social withdrawal, depression, anxiety and interpersonal difficulties (Kittredge 1988; Martin 1984; Zapf 1991). Xavier has clearly matured while living in Barcelona, but his new attitudes towards feelings and relationships on returning home have a deep effect on him.

He sees Martine and says good-bye to her for the final time, kissing her and reminiscing: 'so much has happened between those two kisses, so many convoluted routes'. Xavier wanders aimlessly through the streets of Montmartre and cries for the third time in the film. Again, for the third time, 'No Surprises' plays. Klapisch's choice to set this tearful separation with Martine in Montmartre is canny. It is one of the city's most popular destinations for tourists coming to Paris. Xavier observes that Parisians never go there, telling us that 'I was a foreigner among foreigners'. Klapisch uses a handheld digital camera for this sequence as he tracks Xavier's walk through the Place du Tertre, and it has a quasi-documentary feel to it as passersby look directly at the lens as they notice Romain Duris/Xavier crying.[17]

Xavier then wanders past a café, where a group of foreign students are sitting around a table, speaking several languages at once. 'Erasmus?' he asks them. 'Yes. Why?' they reply, nonchalantly. For Ousselin (2009), this scene is an example of what he terms the 'normalization' of Erasmus, whereby it has become such a culturally ordained rite of passage for a privileged band of European adolescents to spend time in the program that its wider transformative effect is dissipated. Xavier's own personal story is structured in such a way that he believes that he is the only person to have ever benefited from the cultural and linguistic advantages of Erasmus. Yet in fact, his life-changing experience is one of several million; his story is no more and no less exceptional than any other Erasmus student before or since. Yes, the experience has fundamentally transformed him (he has just split up with his girlfriend, seems ready to relate to his long-suffering mother in a more civil manner and is about to abandon his new job to fulfill a lifelong ambition), but it is by no means unique. In this way, Klapisch is subtly undermining the upbeat endings that frequently characterize the American youth film. Our hero has changed but it is a discovery announced somewhat anticlimactically in a muted, understated manner that is neither triumphant nor noteworthy.

At the start of his first day in his new job, Xavier is dressed in a suit and tie. A finicky colleague tells him that 'there is a place for everything' in the office. Neatly arranged yellow, blue and red folders cannot be mixed up. The radiator should be set at level two and no higher. Xavier is a long way from the chaos of the Barcelona apartment here. In keeping with many coming-of-age novels that recount the struggle between the rebellious feelings of the individual and the conformist pressures of society, Xavier abruptly rejects a career at the Ministry of Finance, runs out of the office, along the street (to the sound of Sonia and Selena's 2001 Euro-pop hit '*Que viva la nocha*' ['Live the Night'], back to his room, and starts to write. He has fulfilled his childhood ambition to become a writer, and we have come full circle, back to the start of the film and that first shot of Xavier staring at a blank computer screen and summoning the memories of his time in Barcelona. His experiences in Barcelona have not only changed his understanding about Europe but have also offered a fresh, liberating perspective on his own life. Béguin argues that in this final scene, Xavier is now completely free and can 'take off' (2004: 80). As *The Spanish Apartment* closes, Xavier has a clear notion of what this symbolic take-off now means: 'Now I can tell everything [. . .] After all, it is a story about taking off. It all started here'.

He flicks through photographs of his time in Barcelona. Finally, he declares that now, it's all clear and simple:

> I'm not that. Nor that. I'm no longer that. Nor that. Nor that. Nor that. But I'm all that [looking down at the photos spread out on the floor]. I'm him, him, and him. And him [*image of Alessandro*] and him too [*Tobias*]. And him too [*Lars*]. And I'm him too [*photograph of him as a child*]. [. . .] I'm her [*Soledad*], her [*Wendy*], her, and her too [*Isabelle*]. [. . .] I'm French, Spanish, English, Danish. I'm not one but many. I'm like Europe. I'm all that. I'm a real mess.

This breathless moment of introspective reflection constitutes some of the key lines of the film. As Derakhshani and Zachman (2005: 131) note, 'by the end [. . .] it seems Xavier has become comfortable with, and accepted, the plurality and ambiguity not only of interculturalism but of self as well'. With the advantage of hindsight, Xavier has, finally, reached a level of maturity that allows him to reflect on the benefits of his cultural immersion experience in Barcelona that has not only made him conscious of his own individual identity (and redefined his relationships with his mother, Martine, his professional career, etc.) but also of the deep cultural ties that exist among young people from across Europe. Of equal relevance is the fact that Xavier aligns his lived experiences in a foreign country with people rather than places – the faces of his flatmates are what triggers the final part of his journey towards identity (re)formation. This identification with the other members of the Spanish apartment allegorizes the utopian thrust of the Erasmus program (i.e. the transcending of cultural and linguistic differences) and is the catalyst for the writing of the novel that recounts the events we have just witnessed. That final acceptance by Xavier of the messy reality of his life, and how that life can only ever be rewritten through the interaction with others, is the ultimate mark of his personal growth, change and maturation. There is a freeze-frame on Xavier's smiling face (a visual echo of Truffaut's famous final static image of Antoine Doinel at the sea's edge at the end of *The 400 Blows*). Cue the credits, and Ardag's song '*Cambia la vida*' ('Change your life') accentuates Klapisch's life-affirming message one last time.

Figure 3.5 Antoine Doinel – freeze-framed

Figure 3.6 Xavier Rousseau – freeze-framed again

'The Spanish cocoon'?: A counter-reading

While it is, I think, legitimate to account for Klapisch's positive appraisal of Erasmus and its wider effects on its participants in terms of youthfulness, playfulness and the deferred transition to adulthood and then, in this regard, see *The Spanish Apartment* as an uplifting account of personal transformation and self-actualization in a sun-drenched vibrant city, we need also to offer up a counter-reading of Klapisch's light and bright film. There is a flipside to *The Spanish Apartment* that destabilizes the common reading of the film as a celebration of diversity and a strengthening of intercultural understanding. First, for all the EU's talk of successful student mobility and horizon-broadening experiences, the success of Erasmus program is relative and the takeaway is limited and partial (see Schnitzler and Zemple-Gino 2002; King and Ruiz-Gelices 2003; Morano-Foadi 2005). In 2005–2006, for example, only 1% of all students enrolled at European universities left their home institutions for an Erasmus exchange. During the same period, the scholarship of 150 euros per month for each student had not risen since 1993, thus discouraging applications from students from less favorable financial backgrounds (Lefebvre 2007). Other studies have indicated that Erasmus may actually lead to a decrease in language and intercultural skills (Maiworm 2002; Findlay et al. 2006).

Second, we can critique the privileged milieu that the director explores. The demographics of the students in *The Spanish Apartment* (and the extant literature on Erasmus students bears this out) would seem to suggest that Erasmus attracts a 'privileged', cosmopolitan elite who already identify themselves as 'European'; who have traveled across Europe prior to spending time abroad; who already speak a foreign language, have lived abroad, have friends from other cultures; and who do not belong to ethnic minorities, come from cities or large towns and have parents with higher income. Some critics question the impact of Erasmus on the construction of a European identity at all, arguing, for instance, that it is 'preaching to the converted' (Kuhn 2012: 995). Indeed, it is precisely those students who already feel 'European' who tend to apply for an Erasmus stay in the first place.

Third, much of the Erasmus literature focuses on how foreign exchange students rarely get an opportunity to meet and converse with the locals. When those opportunities do present themselves, the students will tend to portray them 'as a single cultural type' with an emphasis on generalizations about the foreign culture (Papatsiba 2006). When students complete post-Erasmus surveys, they often admit to 'smooth[ing] out all social and interpersonal differences' (112), perhaps reinforcing the guests' resistance to and unwillingness towards interacting with the host. To borrow the term proposed by Fred Dervin and Mari Korpela (2013), the apartment in *The*

Spanish Apartment strongly resembles a 'cocoon community'. This is defined as a group of people who 'gather around a specific purpose [. . .] predominantly on a short-term basis, be it within national boundaries, abroad, transnationally or online [. . .] Members of Cocoon Communities may experience also long-term togetherness; [they] are not necessarily short-lived although they are not viewed as eternal either'. Examples of such communities include seasonal workers, expatriates, online discussion forums and, of most relevance, international students in a foreign city. Its members view belonging to the community as emotionally rewarding; a key characteristic is also its 'involuntary and informal nature' (4).

'Cocoon' is particularly useful in the case of *The Spanish Apartment* because the word conveys protection and home comforts. However, there is another side to the cocoon – a marginal status to the host community, a form of willed retreat from the messy realities of the real world and a strong desire to only establish and maintain exclusive networks with fellow Erasmus students. Papatsiba (2006) argues that for most Erasmus students, regardless of nationality, 'a certain curiosity and desire of encounter with the culturally different Other exist' (108), and yet it is hard to make this case in *The Spanish Apartment*. Isabelle has a relationship with her flamenco teacher, but apart from that, we do not see much interaction between the young people in the flat and the host at all.

These are similar arguments to the ones proposed by Ezra and Sánchez (2005), Pratt (2007) and McCaffrey and Pratt (2011), who all challenge what they regard as Klapisch's superficial treatment of Erasmus, multiculturalism and the ramifications of flow and exchange in 'Fortress Europe'. Ezra and Sánchez in particular question the film's surface-level celebration of transnational European identity, arguing that the flatmates lack psychological depth and 'display little interest in discovering and understanding each other's cultural backgrounds' (144). In turn, Klapisch ignores 'the complex reality that emerges from the relationship between space, history and society' (145). Pratt (2007) also criticizes Klapisch (in *Russian Dolls*) for failing to represent the multiethnicity of Europe or adequately contextualize Xavier's 'national and narrow' parameters; this argument is developed in Pratt again (with McCaffrey 2011) and the way *The Spanish Apartment* controls and sidelines Otherness to shore up heteronormative masculinity and national and sexual conformity. All criticize Xavier for not fully exposing himself to the local culture and Klapisch for serving up 'clichéd capital city dioramas' (2011: 446). Ezra and Sánchez note that he 'fails abysmally' to open up and discover anything other than his native language (142), a point reinforced by McCaffrey and Pratt, who query where Xavier's near-perfect mastery of Spanish by the end of the film has come from (438). On these points, I disagree. Of all the characters in *The Spanish Apartment*, Xavier is the only one to engage with the locals. He is willing to leave the comfort zone of the apartment to wander the streets of Barcelona with Anne-Sophie, negotiating the rent with the Spanish landlord, visiting Juan at the Iposa, and so on. While these may only appear cursory engagements with the local culture, they do at least expose Xavier's growing curiosity and linguistic expertise as well as mark him out as a 'model' Erasmus student.

The affluent cosmopolitanism of *The Spanish Apartment* distances Xavier's travails from much more sustained depictions of the socially varied, multicultural, polyglot versions of French (and European) cultural identity. Yet Klapisch is less concerned with socio-political fidelity than he is with opportunities for individual self-transformation in photogenic European cities. There is always an engagement with current hot-button topics in his cinema, but they are often tackled obliquely or in passing. The trilogy is in fact alive with change as the corollaries of mobility and intercultural (mis) understanding, not to mention the impact of globalization on the emerging adult generation, are contested. It might be unfashionable, but for Klapisch, *The Spanish Apartment* affirms how travel may have a salutary effect on the heart and the mind. By working productively at the interface of genre and auteur cinema, he is offering a 'third way' approach to storytelling that blends youthful exuberance with thoughtful ruminations on where we stand in this increasingly hybridized European society.

Notes

1 *Ce qui me meut* is also the title of Klapisch's short film, shot in 1989.
2 Occasionally, the narrator of the *Bildungsfilm* will reveal early on the end result of the tale they are telling. Stanley Kubrick's *Barry Lyndon* (1975) is a case in point: the two chapter titles – 'By What Means Redmond Barry Acquired the Style and Title of Barry Lyndon' and 'Containing an Account of the Misfortunes and Disasters That Befell Barry Lyndon' – tell us what to expect.
3 *Martine* is the title character in a series of books for children originally written in French by Belgian writers Marcel Marlier and Gilbert Delahaye. The first one, '*Martine à la ferme*' (*Martine on the Farm*), was published in 1954, followed by fifty-nine other books, which have been translated into many different languages. To date, around 100 million copies have been sold.
4 Perrin offers Xavier a '*Donohugue double malt*' – a brand of whisky that, sadly, does not exist.
5 'In any bureaucratic organization there will be two kinds of people: those who work to further the actual goals of the organization, and those who work for the organization itself [. . .] [I]n all cases, the second type of person will always gain control of the organization, and will always write the rules under which the organization functions' (Pournelle 2006). In fact, the application process for European students participating in exchange programs within the EU is relatively straightforward.

6 Fevry's corpus includes *Les Triplettes de Belleville/Belleville Rendezvous* (Sylvain Chomet, 2003), *Les Choristes/The Chorus* (Christophe Barratier, 2004) and *Un long dimanche de fiançailles/A Very Long Engagement* (Jean-Pierre Jeunet, 2004).

7 A graduate from the *ÉNA* (*École Nationale d'Administration*), a prestigious school in France – the school is the principal pathway to senior positions in the French public sector.

8 Coincidentally, in a 2009 interview, Augé declared his love for Barcelona, having visited there several times: 'I like it for various reasons: for the climate, the sea, the light. There are all those colourful walls. Paris is a beautiful city but it's grey; a little sad, in fact. In contrast, Barcelona is completely different [. . .] it's a dynamic, modern city, where many architectural experiments have been made, and at the same time it is a city with an interesting past' (Aragay 2009).

9 (*bon chic, bon genre*/good style, good attitude).

10 In fact, since 2002, this area has been extensively redeveloped and now houses new Barcelona University buildings.

11 Neus returns in *Russian Dolls*, as Xavier's lover in Paris.

12 I wonder if Klapisch was familiar with Danny Boyle's *Shallow Grave* (1994), which contains an almost identical scene in which three flatmates put their prospective roommates through a grueling interview process.

13 Music is important in the film. When Isabelle moves into the apartment, she and Xavier bond over her CDs of Malian singer Ali Farka Touré.

14 Later on, Isabelle tells Xavier: 'What a drag, to be torn between two languages'. Xavier reminds her that it is the similar in Belgium, with Flemish and Walloon, but Isabelle replies 'it's not the same'.

15 The sequence is reminiscent of Mike Figgis's *Timecode* (2000), in which four separate stories unfold simultaneously in real time on a quadruple-split screen and build to a climactic scene in which the stories all converge.

16 Jean-Michel is wearing almost exactly the same clothes at the party as he did at the airport when he first met Xavier – trousers, polo shirt and jacket. Anne-Sophie, in contrast, is now wearing a low-cut, black dress. Xavier does not comment on this in his voiceover, but it is clear that Anne-Sophie too has 'changed' while in Barcelona, a transformation undoubtedly triggered by her affair with Xavier.

17 Jean-Pierre Jeancolas (2005) has noted how the emergence of digital cameras in French cinema has enabled directors to 'approach [their] subject more freely, more incisively and more discreetly' (p. 158).

4   *Russian Dolls* and *Chinese Puzzles*

Revisiting *The Spanish Apartment*

Adolescence is a kind of permanent terminal state.

(Bill Forsyth, director of *Gregory's Girl*
in van Gelder [1982])

Life, for most people, is going from point A to point B. But not for me. I've got a point B problem.

(Xavier, *Chinese Puzzle*)

Russian Dolls synopsis

Set five years after the events of *The Spanish Apartment*, *Russian Dolls* begins in St. Petersburg, where the Barcelona flatmates reunite to attend William's wedding to a Russian ballerina. Through a series of flashbacks, we learn that Xavier and Wendy have become writers, Martine is now a globetrotting environmentalist, and Isabelle a financial journalist. Xavier travels to London to work on a television script with Wendy, and they fall in love. Xavier is unfaithful to Wendy while he ghostwrites the memoirs of Celia (Lucy Gordon), a fashion model in Paris, and they separate. At William's wedding, Wendy and Xavier tentatively reconcile.

Chinese Puzzle synopsis

Set ten years after *Russian Dolls*, Xavier is now forty years old and divorced from Wendy. She decides to move to New York with their two children, and so Xavier moves to Chinatown to be closer to them. While there, he reunites with fellow single parent Martine as well as Isabelle, donating his sperm to her and her Chinese-American partner Ju (Sandrine Holt) so they can become parents. Xavier needs a residency visa to stay in America and so enters into an arranged marriage to a Chinese-American, Nancy (Li Jun Li). He reunites with Martine and persuades her to stay with him in New York.

***

The closing scene of *The Spanish Apartment* saw Xavier recounting the final moments of his *Bildungsroman* in Barcelona. Flecked with a sense of brooding, longing and nostalgia for the past, Xavier's pondering was an explicit indication that his year away from France was one of personal growth and maturation. We last saw him on the runway, arms outstretched, in a freeze-frame, smiling broadly and proclaiming in voiceover, 'It all started here'.

Little did we know that we would meet him, and some of the Barcelona flatmates, two more times over the next eleven years. *Les Poupées russes/Russian Dolls* and *Casse-tête chinois/Chinese Puzzle* return to the same characters when they are in the early thirties and early forties, respectively.[1] Characteristically, Klapisch uses Xavier's specific and localized circumstances as the starting point in both *Russian Dolls* and *Chinese Puzzle* to tangentially examine more substantial issues. All three films 'tell the story of our age, with its ideology of mobility, travel and globalization' (Klapisch 2013). Over the course of these two breezy films, Xavier, Wendy, Isabelle, Martine and William each reminisce about what happened to them in Barcelona and use this introspection as a catalyst towards a greater acceptance of their own conflicting identities and beliefs. Part of the pleasure of the two sequels is to see the long-haul individual trajectories made by familiar characters across an eleven-year period and to see the physical changes in the actors who play them. In a no less striking way than seeing Ethan Hawke, Patricia Arquette, Lorelei Linklater and above all Ellar Coltrane age before our eyes in *Boyhood* (2014, Richard Linklater), it is the changing faces and bodies of Romain Duris and Kelly Reilly in particular that lend an emotional and intimate heft to the narrative experiences of *Russian Dolls* and *Chinese Puzzle*. Klapisch, as Truffaut had done with Jean-Pierre Léaud in the 'Antoine Doinel' cycle, charts the physical transformations of the actors as well as their on-screen moves from adolescent to young adult and from 'thirty-something' to 'forty-something'.[2]

When *The Spanish Apartment* wrapped, Klapisch was certainly not thinking about a sequel or sequels (Klapisch 2014; Klapisch 2017b). Fans and critics often asked him if he would ever go back to the characters, but it was only after the release of his next film, *Not For, or Against (Quite the Contrary)*, in 2003, and having spent some time in St. Petersburg, that Klapisch wrote a screenplay and set about contacting the actors to check their availability. In the case of *Chinese Puzzle*, Klapisch saw an opportunity to revisit the characters for a final time, tie up loose ends and return to a city he spend two years in as a film student in the early 1980s. Klapisch was clearly intrigued by the prospect of following a group of people over a long period of time and periodically revisiting them. In a 2005 interview, he proclaimed himself a fan of documentaries that return to the same people again and again: 'It's an interesting way for cinema to show people getting old and to see their journeys' (Gagnon 2013).[3]

Logistically, production on *Russian Dolls* and *Chinese Puzzle* was more challenging. Whereas *The Spanish Apartment* was written in two weeks, *Russian Dolls* took four months and *Chinese Puzzle* eight months. Actors who were relatively unknown in the summer of 2001 were now recognized European stars, making it difficult to align the schedules of Duris, Tautou, de France and Reilly. The budgets for both films were a lot higher than the 5.3 million € set aside for *The Spanish Apartment* (11 million € for *Russian Dolls*; 18 million € for *Chinese Puzzle*); at the box office, *Russian Dolls* made $24 million, *Chinese Puzzle* $15 million; both attained scores in the 70% range on 'Rotten Tomatoes'. Reviews were generally favorable: Ty Burr called *Russian Dolls* 'something deliciously close to a nature documentary about the young, the foolish, and the alive'; Leslie Felperin praised *Chinese Puzzle* as a 'warm, lovable movie that celebrates cultural pluralism and people's ability to mature'.

As he had done in *The Spanish Apartment*, Klapisch uses a range of techniques to mirror Xavier's experiences in multiple global cities. The 'giddy visual and sonic mélange' (Hornaday 2003) that characterized *The Spanish Apartment* is once again redeployed in inventive ways. Both films are again narrated as a first-person flashback by Xavier and contain non-linear and multiple plotlines, postponed beginnings, fast-forwarding and a choppy editing style. There are scenes in slow-motion, freeze frames, split screens and fantasy sequences (Erasmus paid a visit to Xavier's bedroom in Barcelona; in New York, it is Hegel and Schopenhauer dispensing gnomic *bon mots*); eclectic soundtracks; and inventive credit sequences (the credits for *Chinese Puzzle* contains mosaic-like clips from all three films).

The metaphorical titles are also in place: *Russian Dolls* refers to *matryoshkas*, or Russian nesting dolls. The film is primarily concerned with Xavier's search for the ideal, perfect woman. In voiceover, he tells us: 'We spend our life playing this game, dying to know who will be the last one, the teeny-tiny one hidden inside all the others [. . .] You have to open them one by one, wondering: Is she the last?' In French, a *casse-tête chinois* is a puzzle or brain-teaser; as the name suggests, *Chinese Puzzle* mashes together the different characters' subplots and intersecting timelines. When we saw Xavier freeze-framed at the end of *The Spanish Apartment*, it seems that his particular rite of passage has been completed. But in fact, Xavier did not slip seamlessly into the world of adulthood, preferring instead to reject the security of a job and return to the comfort of his bedroom, recalling photographs and faces of a previous experience. This regressive behavior courses through *Russian Dolls* and *Chinese Puzzle* – life for Xavier has not simplified but become more complex. The complications he faces (professional frustrations, perpetual displacement, romantic intricacies, family responsibilities) are presented by Klapisch as part of a never-ending process of growing up and reaching a level of self-actualization that only gradually benefits both Xavier and those closest to him.

Twists . . .

There are two significant twists in *Russian Dolls*. The first is that Xavier has not become the successful novelist that he/we assumed he would become when he made the decision at the end of *The Spanish Apartment* to pursue his childhood dream and become a writer. This narrative clash is signaled from the outset. One of Xavier's first lines in *Russian Dolls* is 'If I look at my life, it's not impressive'. Klapisch then shows a montage of Xavier surviving on a series of short-term writing jobs. A TV company Xavier writes for tells him to focus on clichés – audiences want 'sunsets and happy ends', a studio boss tells him. The notion of simplistic national stereotypes in *The Spanish Apartment* has now been replaced by a different kind of cliché: populist, commercialized and marketable simulacra of 'happiness' (we can perhaps imagine Klapisch himself being coerced by film financiers to offer up a clichéd facsimile of *The Spanish Apartment* in *Russian Dolls*). Xavier is also employed as a ghostwriter, writing texts for others who take the credit. These notions of (in)authenticity are seeded through the film, especially in Xavier's relationships with women.

Writing, whether daytime soap opera or autobiographical *Bildungsroman*, may yet yield a sense of fulfillment for Xavier. For despite his thirty-something aimlessness, there is clear-sighted realization that writing can create order from chaos. Writing is sorting out the mess of life, Xavier notes, as he sits on a train in front of his laptop. Klapisch then undercuts this moral certainty by showing Xavier in a series of job interviews surrounded by his own doppelgangers playing childlike tunes on a tin pipe behind him.[4] Thus, by avoiding the obvious cliché of starting *Russian Dolls* with Xavier as an immediate success as a writer, Klapisch suggests that Xavier is just as conflicted and chaotic as he was in *The Spanish Apartment*. The path to self-actualization and stable identity will be far more meandering. While Xavier may never reach the level of 'the next Proust', as his editor optimistically describes him in *Chinese Puzzle*, over the course of the trilogy, Xavier ends up 'writing'/'righting' his own life.

Second, of all the returning characters from *The Spanish Apartment*, it is William who has matured the most. In *Russian Dolls*, in a story he tells Xavier in a series of flashbacks, William woos, then marries, Natasha (Evgenia Obraztsova), a Russian ballerina whom he meets while working as a theater technician in London.[5] What is particularly remarkable about this subplot is that the driving factor behind the relationship between William and Natasha is language. When they first meet, they are unable to communicate; he speaks no Russian, she no English. They share one word: '*poka*' (good-bye). When she leaves London, she gives him a piece of paper with her address on it, but it is written in Cyrillic. William is unable to read it, but to continue his budding romance, he spends a year learning Russian before heading off to St. Petersburg to track Natasha down and ask her to marry him. As Jane Warren states, 'we [. . .] are surprised at such a degree of linguistic awareness from the man who in Barcelona was full of clichés about European nationalities, and could hardly speak a coherent word of another language' (2008: 116). Klapisch may be making the same points here about the need for multilingualism and intercultural understanding that he made in *The Spanish Apartment*, but the fact that William has now matured, due perhaps to the redemptive power of the exotic foreigner, indicates how strongly Klapisch believes in the importance of language learning and mobility for Europe's emerging adult generation to sustain and nurture relationships.

That is not to say that William's hardened cultural attitudes are becoming brittle. He still arrives from London at the Gare du Nord train station in Paris and promptly shouts to any French girl that he passes '*Voulez-vous coucher avec moi, ce soir?*' (Do you want to sleep with me tonight?). Old habits die hard. When Wendy comes to St. Petersburg to meet William and Natasha, William acts as translator and de facto cultural ambassador, telling Wendy that the correct word for 'thank you' in Russian is *spassiba*. At the wedding, Tobias, in a speech to the assembled guests, notes the extent of William's metamorphosis: 'When I first met William I thought he was an idiot. Because I'm German, he thought I'm a kind of Nazi [. . .] But today Germany has changed. Russia has changed. And William has changed as well. People can change'. Mireille Rosello has referred to William's 'patience and humility' in *Russian Dolls* (2007: 27) – he has taken steps to learn a language and cross a border that is in turns geographical (London to St. Petersburg via Paris), allegorical (the much sought-after fusion by the EU of 'West' and 'East') and mental (William's shift from immature tourist to proud European native). Coming after the 'bed trick' in Barcelona, Klapisch redeems William a second time – learning a language and embracing alterity has utterly transformed him from 'little Englander' to Euro-citizen.

. . . And (global) turns

Diane Negra states that recent American teen films have been 'particularly concerned with the prospects and limits of mobility' (2007: 199). Similarly, Klapisch's trilogy uses motifs of travel, migration and circulation to bring together or separate his disparate plotlines and comment more broadly on the easy opportunities for border crossings for his protagonists. Mobility is limitless; Xavier can and does go anywhere – and regularly. While the choice of Barcelona for Klapisch was partly autobiographical and partly allegorical, the cities which provide the backdrop for *Russian Dolls* and *Chinese Puzzle* are chosen as examples of hubs, bridges and melting pots. In *Russian Dolls*, the ease of continental travel for these well-heeled, upwardly mobile twenty-somethings that initially brought them to Barcelona is once more replicated. It is telling that one of film's first images is the diagonal whizz of the Eurostar emerging from a tunnel. The image recurs several times during the film, signaling Xavier's shuttling to and from London and Paris as he juggles his professional assignments and increasingly byzantine love life. The wedding in St. Petersburg completes this geographical triangulation and suggests that high-speed train networks, cheap airfares, technological advances and mobile phones have become the hallmarks of the emerging generation that began in *The Spanish Apartment*.

Thematically, the notion of a diverse Europe clearly continues to interest Klapisch:

> *Russian Dolls* is certainly a film on the enlargement of Europe [. . .] the idea was [. . .] to speak of Europe as she has not yet become [. . .]. I have faith in Europe, I'm part of those who believe that the ideal is more important than national problems.

> (Ferenczi 2005: 48)

Chinese Puzzle takes place principally in New York, the ultimate cosmopolitan melting pot. The choice of the city for Klapisch was clear: 'What I like about New York is that it's kind of a metaphor of the rest of the world – there's a neighborhood for every country of the world [. . .] Xavier is really like New York and there's a mirror between his character and the identity of New York' (Douglas 2014). Just as he had done in *The Spanish Apartment*, Klapisch gestures towards the touristic aspects of the city but prefers to focus on the specific geography and iconography of Chinatown. Wendy's vast apartment overlooks Central Park, and Isabelle's Brooklyn rooftop has a view of the Manhattan skyline, but Klapisch and DoP Natasha Braier capture the city's more unfamiliar, less photogenic spaces. Throughout the trilogy, Klapisch films Barcelona, London, New York, Paris and St. Petersburg from above via a series of long aerial shots that map out the physical and emotional terrain onto which the narrative of each film unspools. These shots suggest that physical geography alone does not make a community and that within these bordered districts, suburbs and *arrondissements*, diversity, tension and differences of opinion will often intersect, often messily.

In another visual echo to *The Spanish Apartment*, Xavier moves into Isabelle and Ju's apartment (even carrying his rucksack on his front, as he had done in Barcelona), while he looks for somewhere to live in New York. He ends us sleeping on the sofa and wakes up with a start as Isabelle and Ju eat breakfast (just as he did with Jean-Michel and Anne-Sophie all those years earlier). When he moves into a small flat in Chinatown, he and his children set about decorating it, personalizing it with his own photographs. Xavier finds himself at New York's ground level of marginalized minorities and undocumented migrants, unable (yet) to access Wendy's stable, upmarket, 'adult' lifestyle. But is that lifestyle really something Xavier craves? Klapisch's urgent engagement with macro-issues like globalization, transcontinental relationships and urban construction (as Wendy and Xavier leave the lawyer's office, huge cranes transforming the Manhattan skyline are clearly visible behind them) is juxtaposed with the intimate and restorative affection between Xavier and his children in a sparsely decorated flat as they watch 'The Simpsons' and eat burgers. Klapisch's polyglot saga has always paid close attention to the warp and weft of the enclosed domestic space, and its most intimate moments – whether sharing a steak in Paris or completing jigsaws in London – have often taken place in away from the cacophony of the thrumming metropolis.

This negotiation with global dynamics extends to other aspects of the films – in *Russian Dolls*, Martine attends the World Social Forum in Porto Alegre in Brazil and tells Xavier how 'it really makes you feel connected to the planet'. Her enthusiastic embrace of *altermondialisation* (alternative globalization) and newfound militancy is one way for emerging adults to gain a fierce social conscience and develop stronger links at both the local and global level. By *Chinese Puzzle*, however, Martine has altered her views. She now works for a French tea company, flies into New York for a business appointment with Chinese executives and conducts the entire meeting in fluent Chinese. Once again, suggests Klapisch, language familiarity will prove decisive in our new era of globalized, hyper-connected trade and travel. In *Russian Dolls*, Isabelle has become a financial analyst for a rolling television business channel. Not only is she now using the skills and knowledge she learned in Barcelona for economic and professional ends, but she also symbolizes an alternative path for Klapisch's emerging adults – a secure sense of self provided by meaningful employment. By *Chinese Puzzle*, she has moved to the heart of the global financial sector – Wall Street. McCaffrey and Pratt (2011) had previously read *The Spanish Apartment* and *Russian Dolls* as forms of anti-road movies because their protagonists 'pack their bags, get as far as the crossroads then turn back before even having time to stand in their shoes and wonder' (455). Conversely, by the close of *Chinese Puzzle*, Martine and her children, ready to board the airport shuttle with bags packed, resolve not to return to Paris. Their peripatetic lifestyle, like Xavier's, is (temporarily, at least) over. By each setting down roots in

New York, that *ne plus ultra* of global melting pots, Xavier, Wendy, Isabelle and now Martine have reached their next set of crossroads. They all decide not to go back but to go on.

Xavier

And what, finally, of Xavier? In what ways has he changed since Barcelona? It is often overlooked in the reviews of *The Spanish Apartment* that Xavier at times behaves very poorly in the film: he screams obscenities at his mother (she embodies Xavier's frustration at what he sees as his mundane life in Paris); he is jealous of Wendy, demeans Bruce, threatens to be sexually depraved with Anne-Sophie and is, after all, an adulterer. Those rough edges have not entirely been smoothed down in *Russian Dolls* or *Chinese Puzzle*. His single identity has by now kaleidoscoped into multiple variations: author, husband, lover, father, son, French, European, American. The smile is still there – sometimes glib, sometime needy, sometimes sarcastic – as is the compelling blend of bohemian-bourgeois insouciance and live-by-the-seat-of-your-pants decision-making. In *Russian Dolls*, Xavier vacillates halfheartedly between shop assistant Kassia (Aïssa Maïga), model Celia (Lucy Gordon) and old flame Neus (Irene Montalà). As they work together, he grows attracted to Wendy, and there are still feelings between him and Martine. As one review noted, *Russian Dolls* might just as easily have been called 'Lovers without Borders' (Holden 2006).[6] Fluid gender and identity issues are still at play. At one point, Xavier asks Isabelle to wear a dress and high heels and pretend to be his girlfriend in order to convince his elderly grandfather that he has at last found his future wife. Isabelle reluctantly agrees but forces Xavier in turn to wear a dress and makeup for the benefit of her girlfriends. Klapisch problematizes Xavier's ongoing process of maturation in *Russian Dolls* by setting up the opposition between Wendy and Celia in a fantasy sequence. While in St. Petersburg, he visits the 'Street of Ideal Proportions', whose height and width are identical (22 meters) and its length (220 meters) is exactly ten times its width. Xavier questions whether such harmony is beautiful or mundane and watches a slow-motion version of Celia sashay down the street as if on a catwalk.

These dilemmas about the unattainability of women, and the need to find the 'right one', eventually lead him to realize that imperfection may bring happiness and fulfillment. As per the archetypal plot points of the *Bildungsroman*, Xavier understands that the love of a decent, kind, loving woman can bring contentment. Xavier and Wendy reunite at the end of William's wedding but not before we have seen an argument between Wendy and William's parents after the ceremony. Recalling the similar scene in Maurice Pialat's *Passe ton bac d'abord/Graduate First* (1978), in which the younger generation realize that their parents' generation is just as prone to infidelity and bickering, Xavier and Wendy's cautious union in *Russian Dolls* suggests that while happiness and monogamy might only be transient, it is, for the moment at least, a romantic interlude based not on conflict but on reconciliation.

Towards the end of *Chinese Puzzle*, Xavier sits in a New York subway station with Wendy, Isabelle and Martine. They each tell him the sort of woman he needs:

Wendy: You need a girl who's a little bit fragile, someone who's a shrinking violet, who loves you so much you can manipulate just a little bit.

Isabelle: He likes feisty chicks.

Martine: Xavier plays his cards close to his chest. I think he needs a tough broad. If she's too delicate [. . .]

W.:   Yeah, but sweet. If she's not sweet, if she's too tough, he'll freak out.

M.:   What he really needs is a sensitive girl who's attentive.

I.:   Yeah, but not too clingy. If she's wimpy, he'll suffocate. I can relate to that.

W.:   You need a combination of all three of us.

Figure 4.1 Xavier, Isabelle, Wendy and Martine: fifteen years later

Image courtesy of Photoshot

Over the course of the trilogy, Xavier has fallen for each of these types of women but has never been able to commit to 'the one' (the last doll inside the *matryoshka*). It is only now, staring back at her down the platform, that he realizes that he loves Martine. He implores her to stay in New York so that he and their children might build a life together. She agrees. Not insignificantly, this new union will be forged in the New World, not the Old, amid the graffiti and urban fizz of Chinatown and not the *grands boulevards* of Paris. 'We're going to settle down', Xavier tells Martine. He completes his novel, but his editor is not happy with the 'hideous happy ending'. But Xavier is. He replies, 'When you find happiness, there's nothing more to say. So it's time to stop'. Will he? Won't he? Maybe a fourth film, released around 2023, will reveal all. For this moment, at least, Xavier has grown up.

Notes

1 The timelines are a little off in the two sequels – *Russian Dolls* was made three years after *The Spanish Apartment*, but in the diegetic world the gap is five years; *Chinese Puzzle* is set fifteen years after events in Barcelona but was released eleven years later.
2 Klapisch has not ruled out writing and directing a fourth film, which would see his characters (and actors) enter their fifties (Klapisch 2014).
3 Klapisch does not mention it, but we can presume that he is referring to Michael Apted's series of 'Up' documentaries that has followed the lives of fourteen British children since 1964, when they were seven years old. Apted revisits the subjects every seven years. The most recent installment is due to be shown on British television in 2019, when the subjects will be age 63. In France, the 'Up' series inspired *Que deviendront-ils?/What Will They Become?)*, directed by Michel Fresnel, who filmed the same group of school pupils in Paris from 1984 to 1996.
4 This is a pun for French audiences. A pipe is a '*pipeau*', and the expression '*c'est du pipeau*' means 'to be telling fibs or porkies'. Klapisch leaves us in no doubt about the sincerity of Xavier in these interviews.
5 Obraztsova is a real ballet dancer, spotted by Klapisch at the Mariinsky Ballet in St. Petersburg. She is currently 'prima ballerina' with the Bolshoi Ballet.
6 The principal marketing image for *Russian Dolls* was a picture of Xavier in the center with the faces of the seven women in the film encircling him.

Conclusion

'Life is for the living.
And love is for the giving'[1]

When you're 40 years old, you're not old.

(Klapisch 2014)

And so *The Spanish Apartment* lives on. It's the best publicity the Erasmus scheme ever had. It's Exhibit A for the emerging star persona of Romain Duris. It's the acme of European youth cinema. It remains Cédric Klapisch's best-known film, and the commercial success of the 'Xavier Rousseau' trilogy strengthened his position as an auteur capable of making films at once popular and high-brow, inventive, bitter-sweet and above all sensitive to contemporary issues. The trilogy is three films about time and what happens to people over long periods – how they change, how others perceive them, how the landscape that shapes and defines them alters too.[2] *The Spanish Apartment* has even been reviewed as a haiku: 'Spanish apartment/A group of Europeans/Living in one place/*L'Auberge espagnole*/Watch this film before watching/The *Russian Dolls* film (Hawkes 2011). In the countless press screenings, interviews and masterclasses he has attended since *The Spanish Apartment* was made, Klapisch has always refracted the trilogy through current political circumstances. Back in 2002, he considered himself a 'Europtimist', a passionate advocate for Erasmus and the world-altering perspective travel, mobility and intercultural dialogue could pass onto Europe's 'emerging adult' generation.

In 2005, that utopian view still held relatively firm – Europe needed to expand, to become more inclusive, to bridge East and West, and in the case of Xavier, the redemptive love and unconditional support offered by Wendy at the close of *Russian Dolls* looked ahead to a positive, committed future. Yet by 2013, and *Chinese Puzzle*, those earlier idealistic intentions had become steadily more impracticable, hence the transatlantic turn and the gaze westwards to the New World. Klapisch himself, usually so broadly optimistic about the internal logic of the European project, sensed a waning in the concept of an all-unifying Europeanness: 'the word Europe refers to the word crisis [. . .] austerity has replaced the word euphoria' (2013b). Europe was no longer about cohabitation but the 'Fortress Europe', a traumatic landscape that segregated rich from poor, Europeans from non-Europeans, and citizens from immigrants. Political retrenchment, symbolized by the economic problems of Greece and Spain, and the political conflict in Ukraine (and the subsequent rise of far-right nationalism in Holland, Austria and France), would, for Klapisch in 2017, be accompanied by a conceptual shift in how European youth interacted with each other:

> Today [. . .] this post-*Spanish Apartment* youth [. . .] is extremely reactive. It lives in a form of permanent instantaneousness, in total immersion in social networks. I do not feel that this new form of mobility is as positive as it was fifteen years ago. We have moved into the era of self-love, an inward-looking virtual world.
>
> (Klapisch 2017)

From the un-choreographed hubbub of the Barcelona apartment to the selfie; from real-world curiosity to the echo-chambers of Facebook and Twitter? Perhaps. Or maybe that is the next challenge for European youth films to engage in – to imagine how the nomadic spirit of Xavier and the gang will manage

Figure 5.1 Looking to the future? Xavier 'becomes' an adult

Image courtesy of Photoshot

future encounters with walls both real and symbolic and how the ongoing '*bordel*' of their lives can be recuperated or reshaped by cultural and linguistic encounters both domestic and foreign. And yet it would be remiss in these closing moments to focus solely on the geopolitical and cultural shifts that have taken place in Europe since 2002 and then retrospectively ring-fence *The Spanish Apartment* as a glorious 'moment in time' when Xavier and the EU both faced up to their messy internal contradictions to recreate themselves as outward-looking and receptive bodies, both optimistic for the future.

What the film and its sequels finally propose is a possible road map for navigating the complex terrain of a multilingual, multicultural globalized society in which family and friends, music and food, memory and autobiography can allow, however tentatively, communities and the tensions within them to coexist. Despite his firmly held beliefs about the importance of the European project and the need for it to be sustained and protected, Klapisch does not resort to sloganeering in *The Spanish Apartment*. There are no dogmatic messages or handwringing; instead, he is content to show how, in the saga, idealism slowly gives way to pragmatism. 'Don't look ahead, don't look back' says Xavier to Wendy at the end of *Russian Dolls*. Live in and for the now. The (forty-year-old) kids are all right.

Postscript

In the Brexit referendum of 23 June 2016, 52% of the UK electorate voted to leave the European Union, with the UK on course to leave the EU by March 2019. One area where Britain may now face exclusion is participation in the Erasmus scheme.[3] Post-Brexit, according to the scheme's UK director, Ruth Sinclair-Jones, 'we face a sad moment of uncertainty, after thirty years of this enrichment of so many lives'. Another advocate of Erasmus, Hywel Ceri Jones, who headed up one of the EU's earliest education and training departments in the 1970s, talked of a period of bereavement: '[It is] a tragedy of staggering proportions for universities throughout the country, for the structured internationalization of our academic institutions [. . .] We are talking about enriched and changed lives, lifelong friendships – since the programme was launched, so many Erasmus babies have been born to couples who met through Erasmus'. Whatever happens in the years ahead, whether it is modified bilateral arrangements, exchanges with non-EU countries (Norway, Switzerland) or even the development of a global network of student exchange agreements, it is to be hoped that the rich cultural relations, linguistic and research and development opportunities, and global citizenship understanding that Erasmus has done so much to inculcate in a generation of British students does not disappear in 2019. Said one student, age nineteen, 'It's more important than ever that students take the opportunity to discover new countries and expose themselves to different opinions and cultures. Otherwise we risk becoming really insular' (Williams 2017).

***

In Barcelona, on 17 August 2017, thirteen people were killed and over 130 were injured after a driver deliberately drove a van onto the pavement of the busy tourist precinct of La Rambla and crashed into pedestrians for about 500 meters. Citizens of twenty-four countries were among those killed and injured in the terror attack. In a march through the streets of Barcelona a few days later, half a million people defiantly chanted the words *'No Tinc Por'* (I'm not afraid). Said one demonstrator, age sixty-three, 'We have to know how to speak to each other and understand others. Everyone has to learn how to be more human' (Anon. 2017b)

***

Following a referendum on 1 October 2017, the ruling separatists in the Catalan parliament, led by its president Carles Puigdemont, declared independence from Spain on 27 October. Madrid retaliated by imposing direct rule, stripping Catalonia of its autonomy and forcibly clashing with pro-independence supporters. Over the next few days, hundreds of thousands attended nationwide rallies for Spanish unity and Catalan independence, notably in Barcelona. As of April 2018, Puigdemont remains in a self-imposed exile in Brussels and will be arrested if he returns to Spain. Support among eighteen-to thirty-four-year-old Catalans for the 'Yes' side in the referendum has always remained higher than for the 'No' camp, but not all young people back self-rule. Cristina Sanchez, twenty-one, remains conflicted: 'I feel Catalan [. . .] and Spanish' (Vicente 2017).

Notes

1 Lyrics from closing credits song of *Chinese Puzzle*, 'Love is for . . .' (by Kraked Unit feat. Gary Mudbone Cooper).
2 That obsession with time continues. In *Back to Burgundy* (2017), to establish the changing rhythms of the Burgundy countryside throughout a twelve-month cycle, Klapisch hired a photographer to take a picture of the same tree every day at 3 p.m. for one year.
3 The number of UK students in the scheme rose by 115% between 2007 and 2014.

Bibliography

Note: Several reviews of the film were consulted at the extensive electronic database at the Bibliothèque du Film at the Cinémathèque Française in Paris. The scanning of these reviews has often resulted in the omission or deletion of page numbers (signaled here as n.p.).

Abrams, M. H. (1981) *A Glossary of Literary Terms*, 4th edn, New York: Holt, Rinehart & Winston.

A. C. (2002) '*L'auberge espagnole*', *Les Echos*, 19 June, n.p.

Aitken, I. (2001) *European Film Theory and Cinema: A Critical Introduction*, Bloomington, IN: Indiana University Press.

Alfranseder, E., Fellinger, J., and Taivere, M. (2011) *E-Value-Ate Your Exchange: Research Report of the ESN Survey 2010*, Brussels: Erasmus Student Network.

Amago, S. (2007) 'Todo Sobre Barcelona: Refiguring Spanish Identities in Recent European Cinema', *Hispanic Research Journal*, 8:1, pp. 11–25.

Anatrella, T. (1988) *Interminables adolescences: les 12–30 ans, puberté, adolescence, postadolescence: une société adolescentrique*, Paris: Cerf/Cujas.

Anatrella, T. (2003) 'Les Adulescents', *Études*, 399:7, pp. 37–47.

Anderson, B. (1983) *Imagined Communities*, London & New York: Verso.

Anon. (2003) '*L'Auberge espagnole*: About the Production', *Cinema.com*, online, http://cinema.com/articles/2228/auberge-espagnole-l-about-the-production.phtml (accessed 12 March 2017).

Anon. (2013) 'Interview du réalisateur Cédric Klapisch', *Cinedirectors.net*, online, www.cine-directors.net/interview19.htm (accessed 12 March 2017).

Anon. (2014) 'Interview with Céline Sciamma', *Cineuropa*, online, May, http://cineuropa.org/vd.aspx?t=video&l=en&did=257528 (accessed 12 August 2017).

Anon. (2017a) 'Welcome to the World of Erasmus Exchange!', *Erasmus Programme*, online, www.erasmusprogramme.com (accessed 3 January 2017).

Anon. (2017b) 'Spain Attacks: King Felipe Joins Thousands on Anti-Terrorism March', *The Guardian*, online, 27 August, www.theguardian.com/world/2017/aug/26/spain-attacks-king-felipe-vi-to-join-barcelona-anti-terror-march (accessed 4 February 2018).

Anon. (2018) 'Cédric Klapisch Box Office Figures', *JP's Box-Office*, online, http://jpbox-office.com/fichacteur.php?id=81&view=7 (accessed 4 February 2018).

Antoine, P. (2005) 'Cédric Klapisch, European New Wave', *Café Babel*, online, 17 September, www.cafebabel.co.uk/article/cedric-klapisch-european-new-wave. html (accessed 7 August 2017).

Aragay, I. (2009) 'Interview with Marc Augé: We May Well Fear That the World Is Advancing towards a New Aristocracy', *Barcelona Metropolis*, online, Autumn, https://web.archive.org/web/20110829032124/www.barcelonametropolis.cat/en/ page.asp?id=21&ui=278 (accessed 12 May 2017).

Arnett, J. J. (2004) *Emerging Adulthood: The Winding Road from the Late Teens through the Twenties*, Oxford: Oxford University Press.

Augé, M. (1995) *Non-Places: Introduction to an Anthropology of Supermodernity*, New York & London: Verso.

Austin, G. (2008) *Contemporary French Cinema: An Introduction*, 2nd edn, Manchester: Manchester University Press.

Baker, B. (2003) '*Pot Luck*', in Pym, J. (ed.) *Time Out Film Guide*, 12th edn, London: Penguin, p. 935.

Baudelaire, C. ([1863], 1964) *The Painter of Modern Life and Other Essays*, ed. & trans. J. Mayne, New York: Phaidon.

Beck, U. and Beck-Gernsheim, E. (2002) *Individualization*, London: Sage.

Béguin, O. (2004) '*L'Auberge Espagnole*: Interculturalism in the European: Melting Pot', in Powell, D. and F. Sze (eds.) *Critical Issues in Multiculturalism, Conference Proceedings*, vol. 8, Oxford: Interdisciplinary Press, pp. 71–82.

Bennhold, K. (2005) 'Quietly Sprouting: A European Identity', *The New York Times*, online, 26 April, www.nytimes.com/2005/04/26/world/europe/quietly-sprouting-a-european-identity.html (accessed 16 August 2017).

Berghahn, D. (2010) 'Coming of Age in the Hood: The Diasporic Youth Film and Questions of Genre', in Berghahn, D. and C. Sternberg (eds.) *European Cinema in Motion: Migrant and Diasporic Film in Contemporary Europe*, London: Palgrave Macmillan, pp. 235–255.

Bernstein, J. (1997) *Pretty in Pink: The Golden Age of Teenage Movies*, New York: St. Martin's Press.

Blumenfeld, S. (2002) '*L'auberge espagnole*', *Le Monde*, 19 June, n.p.

Blum-Reid, S. (2009) 'Away from Home? Two French Directors in Search of Their Identity', *Quarterly Review of Film and Video*, 26:1, pp. 1–9.

Blum-Reid, S. (2016) *Travelling in French Cinema*, New York: Palgrave Macmillan.

Boulé, J.-P. (2011) 'Cédric Klapisch's *The Spanish Apartment* and *Russian Dolls* in *Nausea's* Mirror', in Boulé, J.-P. and E. McCaffrey (eds.) *Existentialism and Contemporary Cinema: A Sartrean Perspective*, New York & Oxford: Berghahn, pp. 157–174.

Bradshaw, P. (2003) '*Pot Luck*', *The Guardian*, online, 9 May, www.theguardian. com/culture/2003/may/09/artsfeatures7 (accessed 10 August 2017).

Bradshaw, P. (2008) '*Paris*', *The Guardian*, online, 25 July, www.theguardian.com/ film/2008/jul/25/drama (accessed 10 August 2017).

Brooks, X. (2003) 'Eurostar and the Europudding', *The Guardian*, online, 8 May, www. guardian.co.uk/film/2003/may/08/features.xanbrooks (accessed 19 January 2015).

Byrnes, P. (2003) '*The Spanish Apartment*', *Sydney Morning Herald*, online, 18 December, www.smh.com.au/articles/2003/12/17/1071337018173.html (accessed 10 August 2017).

Charney, M. J. (1996) 'It's a Cold World Out There: Redefining the Family in Contemporary American Film', in Loukides, P. and L. K. Fuller (eds.) *Beyond the Stars 5: Themes and Ideologies in American Popular Film*, Bowling Green, OH: Bowling Green State University Popular Press, pp. 21–42.

Considine, D. (1981) 'The Cinema of Adolescence', *Journal of Popular Film and Television*, 9:3, pp. 123–136.

Considine, D. (1985) *The Cinema of Adolescence*, Jefferson, NC: McFarland.

Coop, E. (2017) 'Magnum's Alex Webb on the Power of Photography', *Dazed Digital*, online, 15 March, www.dazeddigital.com/photography/article/35120/1/magnums-alex-webb-on-the-power-of-photography (accessed 30 June 2017).

da Cunha, A. (2013) 'Dans l'œil de Cédric Klapisch, les couleurs du chaos', *Le Monde*, online, 15 August, www.lemonde.fr/culture/article/2013/08/15/les-couleurs-du-chaos_3462085_3246.html (accessed 3 October 2016).

Danks, A. (2003) 'From St. Kilda to Kings Cross (Almost): Some Observations on the 2003 Sydney Film Festival', *Senses of Cinema*, online, July, http://sensesofcinema.com/2003/festival-reports/2003sydneyff/ (accessed 17 August 2017).

Darras, M. (2002) '*L'Auberge espagnole*', *Positif*, 497–498, July–August, p. 117.

Dawson, T. (2003) '*Pot Luck*', *BBC.co.uk*, online, 30 April, www.bbc.co.uk/films/2003/04/08/pot_luck_2003_review.shtml (accessed 10 August 2017).

de Certeau, M. (1988) *The Practice of Everyday Life*, trans. S. Rendall, Berkeley: University of California Press.

Denby, D. (2003) 'School Days', *The New Yorker*, online, 19 May, www.newyorker.com/magazine/2003/05/19/school-days-6 (accessed 10 August 2017).

Derakhshanim, M. and Zachman, J. A. (2005) 'Une histoire de décollage: The Art of Intercultural Identity and Sensitivity in *L'Auberge espagnole*', *Transitions: Journals of Franco-Iberian Studies*, 1:1, pp. 126–139.

Doherty, T. (1988) *Teenagers and Teenpics: The Juvenilization of American Movies in the 1950s*, Boston: Unwin Hyman.

Douglas, M. (2014) 'Interview: Cedric Klapisch and Romain Duris Conclude a Trilogy with *Chinese Puzzle*', *ComingSoon.net*, online, 15 May, www.comingsoon.net/movies/features/118016-interview-cedric-klapisch-and-romain-duris-conclude-a-trilogy-with-chinese-puzzle (accessed 1 June 2017).

Driscoll, C. (2011) *Teen Film: A Critical Introduction*, Oxford: Berg.

Dubois, A. (2002) '*L'auberge espagnole*', *Les Inrockuptibles*, 18 June, n.p.

Ebert, R. (2003) '*L'auberge espagnole*', *RogerEbert.com*, online, 23 May, www.rogerebert.com/reviews/lauberge-espagnole-2003 (accessed 17 August 2017).

Egloff, K. M. (2007) *Les adolescents dans le cinéma français: entre deux mondes*, Lewiston, NY: Edwin Mellen Press.

E. L. (2002) '*L'auberge espagnole*', *L'Express*, 20 June, n.p.

Elliot, A. and Urry, J. (2010) *Mobile Lives*, New York: Routledge.

European Commission (2015) 'Erasmus: Facts, Figures and Trends', online, ec.europa.eu/dgs/education_culture/repository/.../erasmus-plus-facts-figures_en.pdf (accessed 5 March 2017).

Ezra, E. and Sánchez, A. (2005) '*L'Auberge espagnole* (2002): Transnational Departure or Domestic Crash Landing?', *Studies in European Cinema*, 2:2, pp. 137–148.

Fallon, J. (2007) '*Ni pour, Ni contre*: Conflict and Community in the Films of Cédric Klapisch', *Foreign Language Annals*, 40:2, pp. 201–214.

Ferenczi, A. (2005) 'L'Europtimiste', *Télérama*, 15 June, pp. 48–50.

Fevry, S. (2017) 'Sepia cinema in Nicolas Sarkozy's France: Nostalgia and National Identity', *Studies in French Cinema*, 17:1, pp. 60–74.

Findlay, A., King, R., Stam, A., and Ruiz-Gellices, E. (2006) 'Ever Reluctant Europeans: The Changing Geographies of UK Students Studying and Working Abroad', *European Urban and Regional Studies*, 13:4, pp. 291–318.

Fischer, L. (2017) *Cinema by Design: Art Nouveau, Modernism, and Film History*, New York: Columbia University Press.

Fligstein, N. (2008) *Euroclash: The EU, European Identity, and the Future of Europe*, Oxford: Oxford University Press.

Franco, J. (2017) 'The Difficult Job of Being a Girl: Key Themes and Narratives in Contemporary Western European Art Cinema by Women', *Quarterly Review of Film and Video*, 34:7, pp. 1–15.

Gagnon, M.-J. (2003) 'Cédric Klapisch: de *L'auberge espagnole* au *Casse-tête chinois*', *Taxi-Brousse*, online, 29 December, www.taxibrousse.ca/2013/12/29/entre-lauberge-espagnole-et-les-poupees-russes/ (accessed 3 February 2016).

Gaw, K. F. (2000) 'Reverse Culture Shock in Students Returning from Overseas', *International Journal of Intercultural Relations*, 24:1, pp. 83–104.

George, S. (1990) *An Awkward Partner: Britain in the European Community*, Oxford: Oxford University Press.

Gott, M. (2015) 'After the Wall: Touring the European Border Space in Post-1989 French-Language Cinema', *Transnational Cinemas*, 6:2, pp. 183–205.

Grasset, J.-P. (2002) '*L'auberge espagnole*', *Le Canard enchaîné*, 19 June, n.p.

Green, C. (2014) 'EU's Erasmus Study abroad Progamme Is Responsible for 1 Million Babies', *The Independent*, online, 23 September, www.independent.co.uk/student/news/eus-erasmus-study-abroad-programme-responsible-for-1m-babies-9751749.html (accessed 3 August 2017).

Gronne, V. and Miklaseviciute, D. (2014) 'Erasmus-Little More Than an EU-Subsidized Party?', *EU Observer*, online, 20 May, https://euobserver.com/opinion/124190 (accessed 7 September 2017).

Guilloux, M. (2002) 'Il faut bien que jeunesse s'amuse', *L'Humanité*, online, 19 June, www.humanite.fr/node/267213 (accessed 4 September 2017).

Handyside, F. (2016) 'Emotion, Girlhood, and Music in *Naissance des pieuvres* (Céline Sciamma, 2007) and *Un amour de jeunesse* (Mia Hansen-Løve, 2011)', in Handyside, F. and K. Taylor-Jones (eds.) *International Cinema and the Girl*, New York: Palgrave Macmillan, pp. 121–133.

Hawkes, M. (2011) 'L'Auberge espagnole', *Review Haiku*, 2, n.p.

Henderson, S. (2006) 'Youth, Excess, and the Musical Moment', in Conrich, I. and E. Tincknell (eds.) *Film's Musical Moments*, Edinburgh: Edinburgh University Press, pp. 146–157.

Higbee, W. (2006) '*Diva*', in Powrie, P. (ed.) *The Cinema of France*, London & New York: Wallflower, pp. 153–162.

Holden, S. (2006) 'In *Russian Dolls*, Some Continuing Adventures of Europe's Young Suave Set', *The New York Times*, online, 10 May, www.nytimes.com/2006/05/10/movies/10doll.html (accessed 31 December 2016).

Hopewell, J. (2014) 'Cédric Klapisch: Life Isn't over Until It Ends', *Variety*, online, 16 January, http://variety.com/2014/film/global/cedric-klapisch-life-isnt-over-until-it-ends-1201061902/ (accessed 17 September 2017).

Hornaday, A. (2003) 'L'Auberge: Wow, What a Trip!', *The Washington Post*, online, 23 May, www.washingtonpost.com/wp-dyn/content/article/2003/05/23/AR2005040200649.html (accessed 7 September 2017).

Hughes, R. (2015) *The Spectacle of Skill: New and Selected Writings of Robert Hughes*, New York: Alfred A. Knopf.

Imre, A. (2007) 'The Age of Transition: Angels and Blockers in Recent Eastern and Central European Films', in Shary, T. and A. Seibel (eds.) *Youth Culture in Global Cinema*, Austin: University of Texas Press, pp. 71–86.

Ivan-Zadeh, L. (2017) '*Back to Burgundy*', *The Times*, online, 1 September, www.thetimes.co.uk/article/back-to-burgundy-8xsfkc25b (accessed 7 September 2017).

Jeancolas, J.-P. (2005) 'The Confused Image of *le jeune cinéma*', *Studies in French Cinema*, 5:3, pp. 157–161.

Kammoun-Carlet, M. (1997) 'Chacun cherche l'autre', *Nouvelle Revue Française*, online, May, www.cedricklapisch.com/interviews_uk.html (accessed 4 September 2017).

King, R. and Ruiz-Gelices, E. (2003) 'International Student Migration and the European Year Abroad: Effects on European Identity and Subsequent Migration Behaviour', *International Journal of Population Geography*, 9:3, pp. 229–252.

Kittredge, C. (1988) 'Growing Up Global', *The Boston Globe Magazine*, 3 April, pp. 37–41.

Klapisch, C. (2002a) 'Interview with Hervé', *Ecran Noir*, online, June, http://www.ecrannoir.fr/entrevues/entrevue.php?e=59 (accessed 21 June 2017).

Klapisch, C. (2002b) 'Cédric Klapisch: chacun cherche les autres', Interview with Philippe Piazzo, *Le Monde*, 19 June, n.p.

Klapisch, C. (2002c) 'Interview with Bérénice Balta', *Cinelive*, online, June 2000 [sic], www.cedricklapisch.com/itw/auberge_cinelive_juin2000.html (accessed 12 July 2017).

Klapisch, C. (2012) '25 ans déjà . . .', *Huffington Post*, online, 11 April, www.huffingtonpost.fr/cedric-klapisch/25-ans-deja_b_1414742.html (accessed 12 July 2017).

Klapisch, C. (2013a) 'My Story Tells the Tale of Globalization', Interview with Matthieu Amaré, *Café Babel*, online, 29 November, www.cafebabel.co.uk/culture/article/cedric-klapisch-my-story-tells-the-tale-of-globalisation.html (accessed 12 May 2017).

Klapisch, C. (2013b) '*Casse-tête chinois*: portrait de Xavier, héros européen incarné par Romain Duris', interview with Alexis Ferenczi, *Huffington Post*, online, 12 April, www.huffingtonpost.fr/2013/12/03/casse-tete-chinois-xavier-romain-duris_n_4379010.html (accessed 12 May 2017).

Klapisch, C. (2014) 'Feeling the Pull of New York', Interview with Richard Mowe, *Eye for Film*, online, 16 June, www.eyeforfilm.co.uk/feature/2014-06-16-interview-with-cedric-klapisch-about-chinese-puzzle-feature-story-by-richard-mowe (accessed 12 May 2017).

Klapisch, C. (2017a) 'Les inscriptions en Erasmus ont doublé après *L'Auberge espagnole*', Interview with Elena Scappaticci, *Le Figaro*, online, 10 January, www.lefigaro.fr/cinema/2017/01/09/03002-20170109ARTFIG00257-cedric-klapischles-inscriptions-en-erasmus-ont-double-apres-l-auberge-espagnole.php (accessed 1 September 2017).

Klapisch, C. (2017b) 'I Always Like to Discover and Rediscover the Characters in My Films', Interview with Leo Verswijver, *Film Talk*, online, 21 June, https://filmtalk.org/2017/06/21/back-to-burgundy-with-cedric-klapisch-i-always-like-to-discover-and-rediscover-the-characters-in-my-films (accessed 1 September 2017).

Korpela, M. and Dervin, F. (eds.) (2013) *Cocoon Communities: Togetherness in the 21st Century*, Newcastle Upon Tyne: Cambridge Scholars Publishing.

Kracauer, S. (1960) *Theory of Film: The Redemption of Physical Reality*, London & New York: Oxford University Press.

Krzaklewska, E. (2013) 'ERASMUS Students between Youth and Adulthood: Analysis of the Biographical Experience', in Feyen, B. and E. Krzaklewska (eds.) *ERASMUS Phenomenon: Symbol of a New European Generation?*, Bern: Peter Lang, pp. 79–96.

Krzaklewska, E. and Krupnik, S. (2007) *Exchange Students' Rights*, Brussels: Erasmus Student Network.

Kuhn, T. (2012) 'Why Educational Exchange Programmes Miss Their Mark: Cross-Border Mobility, Education and European Identity', *Journal of Common Market Studies*, 50:6, pp. 994–1010.

Lefebvre, J.-S. (2007) 'Erasmus Turns 20: Time to Grow Up?', *Café Babel*, online, 22 January, www.cafebabel.co.uk/politics/article/erasmus-turns-20-time-to-grow-up.html (accessed 7 September 2017).

Lewis, J. (1992) *The Road to Romance and Ruin: Teen Films and Youth Culture*, New York: Routledge.

Liz, M. (2015) 'From European Co-Productions to the Euro-Pudding', in Harrod, M., M. Liz and A. Timoshkina (eds.) *The Europeanness of European Cinema: Identity, Meaning, Globalization*, London & New York: I.B. Tauris, pp. 73–86.

Liz, M. (2016) *Euro-Visions: Europe in Contemporary Cinema*, London & New York: Bloomsbury.

Loiseau, J.-C. (2002) '*L'auberge espagnole*', *Télérama*, 19 June, n.p.

Lucia, C. (2009) 'The Many Faces of Paris: An Interview with Cédric Klapisch', *Cineaste*, 35:1, online, www.cineaste.com/winter2009/the-many-faces-of-paris an-interview-with-cdric-klapisch/ (accessed 1 February 2016).

Maiworm, F. (2002) 'Erasmus: Continuity and Change in the 1990s', *European Journal of Education*, 36:4, pp. 459–472.

Malausa, M. (2002) '*L'Auberge espagnole*', *Cahiers du cinéma*, 569, June, p. 86.

Martin, A. (1994) 'Teen Movies: The Forgetting of Wisdom', in *Phantasms*, Ringwood: McPhee Gribble, pp. 63–69.

Martin, J. N. (1984) 'The Intercultural Reentry: Conceptualization and Directions for Future Research', *International Journal of Intercultural Relations*, 8:2, pp. 115–134.

Massallé, L. (2014) 'Strength, Balance, Courage and Common Sense', *Barcelona Cultural News*, online, 16 November, https://barcelonaculturalnews.wordpress.com/2014/11/16/strength-balance-courage-and-common-sense/ (accessed 2 August 2017).

Mayne, J. (2005) 'Tous les garçons and toutes les filles', *Studies in French Cinema*, 5:3, pp. 201–218.

Mazdon, L. (2001) 'Space, Place and Community in *Chacun cherche son chat*', in Mazdon, L. (ed.) *France on Film: Reflections on Popular French Cinema*, London: Wallflower, pp. 95–105.

McCaffrey, E. and Pratt, M. (2011) 'Erasmus, Exchange Value and Euronormativity in Cédric Klapisch's *L'auberge espagnole* and *Les poupées russes*', in McCormack, J., M. Pratt and A. Rolls (eds.) *Hexagonal Variations: Diversity, Plurality and Reinvention in Contemporary France*, Amsterdam: Rodopi, pp. 433–455.

Mereu-Boulch, L. (2002a) 'Je suis flemmard [*I'm lazy*]', Interview with Romain Duris, *France-Soir*, 19 June, n.p.

Mereu-Boulch, L. (2002b) '*L'auberge espagnole*', *France-Soir*, 19 June, n.p.

Mitchell, K. (2015) 'Rethinking the Erasmus Effect on European Identity', *Journal of Common Market Studies*, 53:2, pp. 330–348.

Moine, R. (2015) 'Contemporary French Comedy as Social Laboratory', in Fox, A., M. Marie, R. Moine and H. Radner (eds.) *A Companion to Contemporary French Cinema*, Chichester: John Wiley and Sons, pp. 233–255.

Morano-Foadi, S. (2005) 'Scientific Mobility, Career Progression, and Excellence in the European Research Area', *International Migration*, 43:5, pp. 134–160.

Morrey, D. (2016) 'The Rough and the Smooth: Narrative, Character and Performance in *Fingers* (1978) and *De battre mon coeur s'est arrêté/The Beat That My Heart Skipped* (2005)', *Studies in French Cinema*, 16:3, pp. 190–204.

Nacache, J. (2005) 'Group Portrait with a Star: Jeanne Balibar and French 'jeune' cinema', *Studies in French Cinema*, 5:1, pp. 49–60.

Nacache, J. (2015) 'Was There a Young French Cinema?', in Fox, A., M. Marie, R. Moine and H. Radner (eds.) *A Companion to Contemporary French Cinema*, Chichester: John Wiley and Sons, pp. 184–204.

Neale, S. (2007) 'Teenpics', in Cook, P. (ed.) *The Cinema Book*, 3rd edn, London: BFI, pp. 367–373.

Negra, D. (2007) 'An American Werewolf in London', in Merck, M. (ed.) *America First: Naming the Nation in US Film*, London: Routledge, pp. 199–213.

Nettelbeck, C. (1999) 'In a Distinctive Cinema Culture', *Australian Journal of French Studies*, 36:1, pp. 3–11.

O'Sullivan, M. (2003) 'L'auberge: Group Dynamite', *The Washington Post*, online, 23 May, www.washingtonpost.com/wpdyn/content/article/2003/05/23/AR2005033117438.html (accessed 7 September 2017).

Ousselin, E. (2009) 'Vers une banalisation des instances européens: *L'Auberge espagnole*', *French Review*, 82:4, pp. 748–761.

Palmer, T. (2011) *Brutal Intimacy: Analysing Contemporary French Cinema*, Middletown, CT: Wesleyan University Press.

Palmer, T. (2015) 'Modes of Masculinity in Contemporary French Cinema', in Fox, A., M. Marie, R. Moine and H. Radner (eds.) *A Companion to Contemporary French Cinema*, Chichester: John Wiley and Sons, pp. 419–438.

Papatsiba, V. (2006) 'Study abroad and Experiences of Cultural Distance and Proximity: French Erasmus Students', in Byram, M. and A. Feng (eds.) *Living and Studying abroad: Research and Practice*, Clevedon: Multilingual Matters, pp. 108–133.

Plisken, F. (2002) '*L'auberge espagnole*', *Le Nouvel Observateur*, 20 June, n.p.

Pomerance, M. and Gateward, F. (2005), 'Introduction', in Pomerance, M. and F. Gateward (eds.) *Where the Boys Are: Cinemas of Masculinity and Youth*, Detroit: Wayne State University, pp. 1–18.

Pournelle, J. (2006) 'Chaos Manor Mail', *Jerrypournelle.com*, online, 3 April, www.jerrypournelle.com/archives2/archives2mail/mail408.html#Iron (accessed 7 September 2017).

Powrie, P. (1999) *French Cinema in the 1980s: Nostalgia and the Crisis of Masculinity*, Oxford: Oxford University Press.

Pratt, M. (2007) 'Introduction II: On Being Optimistically European: Modelling Creolization, Cosmopolitanism and Community', *Culture, Theory and Critique*, 48:1, pp. 11–24.

Riotta, G. (2012) 'It's Culture, Not War, That Cements European Identity', *The Guardian*, online, 27 January, www.theguardian.com/world/2012/jan/26/umberto-eco-culture-war-europa (accessed 1 September 2017).

Rosello, M. (2007) 'Imagining European Subjects as Chaotic Borders: Cédric Klapisch's *Pot Luck* and *The Russian Dolls*', in Barriales-Bouche, S. and M. Attignol Salvodon (eds.) *Zoom In, Zoom Out: Crossing Borders in Contemporary European Cinema*, Newcastle Upon Tyne: Cambridge Scholars Publishing, pp. 16–33.

Rouyer, P. and Vassé. C. (2005) 'Entretien avec Jacques Audiard: Et si tuer quelqu'un au cinéma, c'était difficile?', *Positif*, 529, pp. 21–25.

San Miguel, H. and Torres, L. J. (2013) *World Film Locations: Barcelona*, Bristol: Intellect.

Schatz, T. (1981) *Hollywood Genres: Formulas, Filmmaking, and the Studio System*, New York: Random House.

Schnitzler, K. and Zemple-Gino, M. (2002) *Euro Student: Social and Economic Conditions of Student Life in Europe 2000*, London: Longman.

Scott, A. O. (2003) '*L'Auberge espagnole*', *The New York Times*, online, 16 May, www.nytimes.com/movie/review?res=950DE3DA163EF935A25756C0A9659C8B63&mcubz=3 (accessed 1 September 2017).

Shary, T. (1997) 'The Teen Film and Its Methods of Study', *Journal of Popular Film and Television*, 25:1, pp. 38–45.

Shary, T. (2005) *Teen Movies: American Youth on Screen*, London: Wallflower.

Shary, T. (2007) 'Introduction: Youth Culture Shock', in Shary, T. and A. Seibel (eds.) *Youth Culture in Global Cinema*, Austin: University of Texas Press, pp. 1–6.

Shields, J. (2007) *The Extreme Right in France: From Pétain to Le Pen*, London: Routledge.

Shoard, C. (2010) 'Romain Duris: Hero or Antihero?', *The Guardian*, online, 25 June, www.theguardian.com/film/2010/jun/24/romain-duris-heartbreaker-interview (accessed 3 June 2017).

Soulez, G. (2015) 'Moving between Screens: Television and Cinema in France, 1990–2010', in Fox, A., M. Marie, R. Moine and H. Radner (eds.) *A Companion to Contemporary French Cinema*, Chichester: John Wiley and Sons, pp. 96–116.

108   *Bibliography*

Speed, L. (1998) 'Tuesday's Gone: The Nostalgic Teen Film', *Journal of Popular Film and Television*, 26:1, pp. 24–33.

Stratton, D. (2009) '*The Spanish Apartment* Review: A Charming Film', *SBS. com.au*, online, 1 January, www.sbs.com.au/movies/review/spanish-apartment-review-charming-film (accessed 1 September 2017).

Teichler, U. (2002) 'ERASMUS in the SOCRATES Programme: Findings of an Evaluation Study', in *ACA Papers on International Cooperation in Education*, Bonn: Lemmens.

Trémois, C.-M. (1997) *Les Enfants de la liberté: le jeune cinéma français des années 90*, Paris: Editions du Seuil.

Vanderschelden, I. (2007) *Amélie*, London: I.B. Tauris.

Van Gelder, V. (1982) 'Brewed in Scotland: A Prize Comedy', *The New York Times*, online, 23 May, www.nytimes.com/1982/05/23/movies/brewed-in-scotland-a-prize-comedy.html?pagewanted=all (accessed 10 August 2017).

Van Hoeij, B. (2017) '*Back to Burgundy*', *Hollywood Reporter*, online, 16 June, www.hollywoodreporter.com/review/back-burgundy-ce-qui-nous-lie-1012522 (accessed 19 June 2017).

Van Mol, C. and Timmermann, C. (2014) 'Should I Stay or Should I Go? An Analysis of the Determinants of Intra-European Student Mobility', *Population, Space and Place*, 20:5, pp. 465–479.

Van Mol, S. (2013) 'Intra-European Student Mobility and European Identity: A Successful Marriage?', *Population, Space and Place*, 19:2, pp. 209–222.

Vasse, D. (2008) *Le Nouvel Âge du cinéma d'auteur français*, Paris: Klincksieck.

Verstraete, G. (2010) *Tracking Europe: Mobility, Diaspora, and the Politics of Location*, Durham, NC: Duke University Press.

Vicente, A. (2017) 'Catalan Youths Drive Push for Independence from Spain', *The Local Es*, online, 12 September, www.thelocal.es/20170912/catalan-youths-drive-push-for-independence-from-spain (accessed 4 February 2018).

Vincendeau, G. (2001) 'Café Society', *Sight and Sound*, 11:8, pp. 22–25.

Vincendeau, G. (2007) 'From *La Cage aux rossignols* (1945) to *Les Choristes* (2004): Changes and Continuities in French Popular Cinema', in Waldron, D. and I. Vanderchelden (eds.) *France at the Flicks: Trends in Contemporary French Popular Cinema*, Newcastle Upon Tyne: Cambridge Scholars Publishing, pp. 63–74.

Wakeman, J. (1988) 'Eric Rohmer', in *World Film Directors, Volume 2, 1945–1985*, New York: H. W. Wilson, pp. 919–928.

Walters, B. (2003) '*Pot Luck*', *Sight and Sound*, 13:7, p. 55.

Warren, J. (2008) 'Giving Voice to Multilingual Europe in Contemporary European Cinema', in Warren, J. and H. Merle Benbow (eds.) *Multilingual Europe: Reflections on Language and Identity*, Newcastle Upon Tyne: Cambridge Scholars Publishing, pp. 107–126.

Wenders, W. (2010) 'Image and Identity of Europe: The Role of Cinema and of Film Literacy', online, http://ec.europa.eu/culture/archive/sources_info/studies/pdf/exec_summary_en.pdf (accessed 1 July 2017).

White, P. E. (2005) 'Portrait of the Artist as a Young Boy: François Truffaut, Antoine Doinel, and the Wild Child', in Pomerance, M. and F. Gateward (eds.) *Where the*

Boys Are: Cinemas of Masculinity and Youth, Detroit: Wayne State University, pp. 217–232.

Williams, J. (2017) 'A Student's Plea to Brexit Negotiators: Keep the Erasmus Scheme', *The Guardian*, online, 8 February, www.theguardian.com/education/2017/feb/07/a-students-plea-to-brexit-negotiators-keep-the-erasmus-scheme (accessed 4 February 2018).

Wilson, E. (1999) *French Cinema since 1950: Personal Histories*, London: Duckworth.

Zapf, M. K. (1991) 'Cross-Cultural Transitions and Wellness: Dealing with Culture Shock', *International Journal for the Advancement of Counselling*, 14:2, pp. 105–119.

Zion, L. (2003) '*The Spanish Apartment*', *The Age*, online, 18 December, http://fddp.theage.com.au/articles/2003/12/17/1071337012672.html?from=storyrhs (accessed 10 August 2017).

Žukauskien, R. (2016) 'The Experience of Being an Emergent Adult in Europe', in Žukauskien, R. (ed.) *Emerging Adulthood in a European Context*, New York: Routledge, pp. 3–16.

Index

112   *Index*

Printed and bound by CPI Group (UK) Ltd, Croydon, CR0 4YY
11/04/2025
01843992-0004